The **NO-NONSENSE GUIDE** to the

UNITED NATIONS

Maggie Black

'Publishers have created lists of short books that discuss the questions that your average [electoral] candidate will only ever touch if armed with a slogan and a soundbite. Together [such books] hint at a resurgence of the grand educational tradition... Closest to the hot headline issues are *The No-Nonsense Guides*. These target those topics that a large army of voters care about, but that politicos evade. Arguments, figures and documents combine to prove that good journalism is far too important to be left to (most) journalists.'

Boyd Tonkin,
The Independent,
London

About the author
Maggie Black is an independent writer and editor specializing in international development issues. She belonged to the international civil service from 1977-88 when she worked for UNICEF, initially as an information officer in East Africa, and then as Editor of UNICEF Publications. Since she left the UN system, she has been employed as a consultant on major studies, reports and policy papers for UNDP, WHO, ILO, the World Bank, UNRISD, OHCHR and UNICEF, and for a number of international NGOs. Her books include *The Children and the Nations* (Macmillan and UNICEF, 1987); *A cause for our times* (OUP and Oxfam 1992); *Children First: The story of UNICEF* (OUP 1996); *Water: A matter of life and health* (OUP India, 2005); and *The Last Taboo: Opening the door on the global sanitation crisis* (Earthscan, 2008). She has also been an editor of the *New Internationalist* magazine, and is the author of the *No-Nonsense Guide to International Development* (NI 2007) in this series.

Other titles in the series
The No-Nonsense Guide to Animal Rights
The No-Nonsense Guide to Climate Change
The No-Nonsense Guide to Conflict and Peace
The No-Nonsense Guide to Fair Trade
The No-Nonsense Guide to Globalization
The No-Nonsense Guide to Human Rights
The No-Nonsense Guide to International Development
The No-Nonsense Guide to International Migration
The No-Nonsense Guide to Islam
The No-Nonsense Guide to Science
The No-Nonsense Guide to Sexual Diversity
The No-Nonsense Guide to Tourism
The No-Nonsense Guide to World Health
The No-Nonsense Guide to World History
The No-Nonsense Guide to World Poverty

About the New Internationalist
The **New Internationalist** is an independent not-for-profit publishing co-operative. Our mission is to report on issues of global justice. We publish informative current affairs and popular reference titles, complemented by world food, photography and gift books as well as calendars, diaries, maps and posters – all with a global justice world view.

If you like this *No-Nonsense Guide* you'll also love the **New Internationalist** magazine. Each month it takes a different subject such as *Trade Justice*, *Nuclear Power* or *Iraq*, exploring and explaining the issues in a concise way; the magazine is full of photos, charts and graphs as well as music, film and book reviews, country profiles, interviews and news.

To find out more about the **New Internationalist**, visit our website at
www.newint.org

The **NO-NONSENSE GUIDE** to the

UNITED
NATIONS

Maggie Black

The No-Nonsense Guide to the United Nations
Published in the UK in 2008 by New Internationalist™ Publications Ltd
55 Rectory Road
Oxford OX4 1BW, UK
www.newint.org
New Internationalist is a registered trade mark.

Cover image: Luc Gnago/Reuters/Corbis

Series editor: Troth Wells
Design by New Internationalist Publications Ltd.

 Printed on recycled paper by T J Press International, Cornwall, UK
who hold environmental accreditation ISO 14001.

British Library Cataloguing-in-Publication Data.
A catalogue record for this book is available from the British Library.

Library of Congress Cataloguing-in-Publication Data.
A catalogue for this book is available from the Library of Congress.

ISBN 978-1-904456-88-9

CONTENTS

Foreword

THE HISTORY OF the human race is a history of communities: families that became groups, groups that became tribes, tribes that became societies and societies that became nations. In the new millennium, we have to face the consequences of the failure so far, in spite of two heroic efforts in the 20th century, to create a structured multinational community. Globalization has transformed the way we communicate, trade, travel and view the world, but it has not yet developed a uniting strength in culture, religion or politics. The highest level of real decision-making remains national, for all the alliances and unions between nations generated during the 20th century. The United Nations, the greatest experiment so far in supra-national activity, remains a work in progress.

Only when I became the UK's Permanent Representative to the UN in New York from 1998 to 2003 did I realize how little I knew about the way our only global organization works. If that was the case for a professional diplomat of 30 years' experience, who had worked on many issues which involved the UN as forum, norm-setter, agency and adviser, then how could people with fewer such opportunities be expected to understand the true nature of this extraordinary body? I set myself the target, once 2003 brought retirement, of writing an account of the United Nations I had come to respect, so that anyone interested as a global citizen had a chance to see more clearly what the UN can – and, just as importantly, cannot – achieve in the service of the global community.

That objective was thwarted by the invasion of Iraq in 2003 and its subsequent administration by a US-led coalition of states who claimed, unconvincingly and unsuccessfully, to be acting in the name of the international community as a whole. I was asked to suspend my retirement and go to Baghdad to help steer the coalition's efforts towards an acceptable outcome for the new Iraq. I found that the task was too big for the planning and resources committed to it; and the enterprise left both Iraq and the United Nations more damaged than they would have been if we had chosen a more consensual route to meeting Saddam Hussein's challenge.

So what is the United Nations? What are its compo nent parts and how do they operate? Who owns the organization and to whom is it accountable? What are its true capabilities? This *No-Nonsense Guide* provides an excellent start to answering those questions, and many others: about the origins of the UN after the Second World War – itself a product of the failure of its predecessor, the League of Nations; about the relationship between the member nations of the UN, and the Secretariat and agencies which carry out its work; about the limits of the effectiveness of the Security Council; about the tension between the need for international action on conflict and poverty and the rights of sovereign countries to run their own affairs without outside interference; about the suspicions and misunderstandings between the powerful and the weak; indeed about a whole range of human failings played out at the global level.

Yet the achievements of the UN, and the role it plays in a global society which increasingly disregards borders, also have to be appreciated. With its help, we are gradually learning to address the competitive and conflictual motivations of human societies. It is hard to get our minds around the fact that we cannot only see into the business of every other community on earth, we also have the capacity to destroy it by human action. We need norms, laws, structures and compromises to keep the world secure for humans and other species to live and progress. In that sense, every member of every nation has an investment in the United Nations. We may not feel the immediate effects of failing to keep that investment paid up, but our society will in the longer term. Even the strongest nation cannot protect all its interests, or survive indefinitely, without international help and understanding. How these interests can be accommodated will be the great story of this century; and anyone with a sense of global identity needs to know how that story can best unfold in a positive direction.

Maggie Black has written earlier *No-Nonsense Guides* to international issues, as well as books on water, development and children's rights. Her straightforward, readable approach to the United Nations provides a valuable opportunity to comprehend the gap between the reality and the perception of the UN, and what may be needed to make it effective in the most difficult areas of international misunderstanding. I hope that as many people as possible will read it, and become aware of the huge mistake we shall be making if we do not nurture and improve this essential foundation for the next stage of human evolution.

Sir Jeremy Greenstock
Director of the Ditchley Foundation
UK Permanent Representative to the UN 1998-2003

Introduction

ANYONE WHO WRITES about the United Nations carries a particular set of baggage, often including a stack of prejudices and a love-hate relationship with a body which seems to do and be so much less than it ought. I am no different, so it may help the reader to know where I am coming from.

In the last 30 years, I have seen a great deal of UN development work at first hand – in the field proper, not just country offices. For 11 years I was on UNICEF's staff, first in eastern Africa where I traveled and wrote about programs in many countries, subsequently in New York. As Chairperson of UNICEF's Global Staff Association, I learned a lot about staffing and management issues. While at UNICEF I also wrote my first book, *The Children and the Nations*, about the evolution of its work within the wider UN and international context. Since I became independent, I have undertaken many UNICEF assignments, and others for WHO, UNDP, ILO, UNRISD, the World Bank and UN Human Rights institutions.

If I had joined the system when younger and less worldly, I might have left within months. There were moments of intense disillusion, but I have never lost faith in what its diverse organizations and the committed among its officers – especially in UNICEF, which I know best – manage to do. The reason I wanted to explain this vast and complex institutional machinery via a *No-Nonsense Guide* is that many UN cynics do not understand the first thing about how it works, or the relationships between the UN proper and the rest of its parts. They bundle all UN organizations together, and think the whole lot are tainted by every last story of bumbling bureaucracy, scandal, inertia, and international staff living easy. One of the most important things I wanted to put across is that this set of organizations is not monolithic but multi-structured, and cannot be tarred with one brush.

Among the things I do deplore are the lack of contact between many staff and the realities of life for those that UN programs are trying to assist. Many documents are written in a prose of synthesized banality – to satisfy donors and remove all possible bones of contention – which has to be read to be believed. 'Communications' output may take the form of infotainment, implying that dealing with complex issues is easy as pie. Then there are too many magisterial 'global reports', contributing to the false impression that problems only susceptible to local solutions can be effectively addressed in the ether.

But when all is said and done, a huge amount of experience and effort has gone into building an enormously valuable set of international institutions. My bottom-line prejudice is in favor. And when people criticize 'the UN' for what cannot be achieved because the nations that instruct its institutions will not let them, I am prepared to defend the UN system with every argument I can muster.

Maggie Black
Oxford

1 Great expectations

The Charter of the United Nations was signed on 26 June 1945, bringing into being a new set of institutions to 'end the scourge of war' and promote international co-operation. The Cold War soon deflated their political promise, but the institutions took shape and permanence, and a growing range of other organizations joined or emerged under the UN canopy. Over time, the UN has been subjected to vituperation, partly on the grounds that it has failed to meet the idealized expectations surrounding its birth. What actually is the 'United Nations'? Does it exemplify a moral world order with an independent identity and executive reach of its own, or is it simply a set of forums where nations debate?

IN APRIL 1945, delegates from 50 nations assembled in San Francisco to finalize the contours of a new set of international institutions. These were replacements for the League of Nations, formed in 1919 as part of the peace arrangements following the First World War and overtaken by paralysis at the onset of the Second. The name 'United Nations' had originally been coined in 1942 to describe what history has passed down to us as 'the Allies', the countries victorious in the 1939-45 war, as opposed to the defeated Axis powers. None of the latter could conceivably have been present at San Francisco since the war was not yet over. And at San Francisco, far from aiming to be all-inclusive, the delegates by universal acclamation denied them – together with Franco's Spain – any prospect of membership of the incipient 'World Organization'.[1]

After nine weeks of delays, hesitations and deadlocks, the delegates finally agreed to the wording of the new 'World Security Charter'. Only the Russians insisted on sending the text to be cleared back home in

Moscow: every other delegation had authority to sign on the spot. In a ceremony that began at 6.00am on 26 June and took until the early afternoon, under lights trained on a large round table in the San Francisco Opera House, 200 delegates appended their signatures to the treaty in its five official languages. China, in the person of Dr Wellington Koo of the Nationalist administration, signed first, on the grounds that China had been struggling against oppression by an imperialist aggressor (Japan) longer than anyone else, and no-one wanted Perón's neo-fascist Argentina (alphabetically the first in line) to have the honor – a bellwether of the sensitivities surrounding the smallest UN action. San Francisco took place, incidentally, just months before the armed renewal of China's civil war, leading to the Nationalists' exodus to Formosa (Taiwan), and a longstanding and bitter dispute over China's representation at the new world body.

After the signing, representatives of the five 'Great Powers' (China, France, Russia, Britain and the US) and of some smaller ones – King Feisal of Iraq, Jan Masaryk of Czechoslovakia, General Smuts of South Africa were among these minor figures – briefly spoke, and then came US President Harry Truman. Truman had taken over at the White House on the death of Franklin D Roosevelt only weeks before, and this was his first major public occasion. In ringing tones he captured the optimism of the moment: 'Upon our decisive action rests the hope of those who have fallen, those now living, those yet unborn – the hope for a world of free countries with decent standards of living, which will work and co-operate in a friendly, civilized community of nations... Let us not fail to grasp this supreme chance to establish a worldwide rule of reason, to create an enduring peace under the guidance of God.' When the President finished speaking, 'cheers echoed and re-echoed through the crowded Opera House'.[2]

A climactic moment

The first draft of the Charter had been drawn up at an earlier conference at Dumbarton Oaks, Washington DC, in August 1944. Grousers regretted that the final document was longer, and 'far from perfect'. Nonetheless, it was in the main rapturously received, being described by figures such as ex-President Herbert Hoover as a 'Magna Carta of peace and security for mankind', and a 'turning point in the history of civilization'.[3] In contrast to the 1919 Covenant of the League of Nations, which the US never ratified, the UN Charter was immediately accepted by the US Senate.

Despite all the stumbling blocks, the exercise in multilateral diplomacy at San Francisco was depicted at its climax as a triumph of unanimity. Looking back, that verdict can be seen as an understatement of monumental scale. The Charter was printed in the London *Times* of 27 June and occupied little more than a page. Compare the recent attempt to draw up a new common basis for the European Union, and it is a miracle of brevity. Compare also the nine weeks of negotiation, and – other than the Russians – the delegates' powers to sign on behalf of their governments, and one begins to appreciate that nothing like this could possibly happen today.

Thus was the collectivity of institutions thereafter known as the United Nations flung up on a wave crest of history. The San Francisco conference had opened before the capitulation of Germany, while Hitler was cowering in Berlin, and it finished its business while the Battle of Okinawa still raged. The years of carnage and devastation had created a powerful impetus to build the world anew – an impulse in the popular and political mind that, whatever the real prognostications for consensual 'international security', no-one could gainsay. Crises were ongoing in the Middle East and Poland, which could have easily derailed discussions in the San Francisco drafting committees. Stalin only agreed to the veto procedures for votes in the Security Council after a special emissary had been sent from Washington to persuade him not to cast himself as the incipient UN's wrecker. Palpably, a unique moment produced the circumstances for such an international treaty to be agreed – a truism often repeated, but whose reality only comes home when the tumultuous events of the time are fully recalled.

Naïve though the great expectations surrounding its passage unquestionably were, can we fault its creators for their idealism? The Charter has never been repealed or substantively amended, and to this extent has stood the test of time. No-one would claim that its high ideals have invariably or even regularly been met, and its cadences today carry more than a whiff of anachronism. But equally, in the multiple games of international diplomacy that it has subsequently sanctioned, its articles and the morals they exemplify have proved highly relevant to the conduct of international affairs. It is also true that the time to make reforms in the institutions it created has long passed – notably in the transcendent role of the 'Big Five' or 'Great Powers' who earned their place by winning the 1939-45 war. But in the babble of disputation about which nations in a very different world should share their predominance and on what terms, that reform has not subsequently proved possible.

So what actually was the new set of institutions that the Charter brought into being? And do they fully describe what we understand to be the 'United Nations', or are they just one group of components of a more complex creature? The machinery put in place by the UN's founders is still there, still forming and re-forming, still spawning new sub-sets of itself, to address issues that were nowhere on the horizon in 1945. Surely, that in itself is a major achievement in international affairs. But is it enough?

Interpreting the Charter

The Charter's contents cannot be understood outside their context. The primary concern of the 'Big Three' – Britain, the US and the USSR – was to put in place mechanisms that could be used to prevent another global conflagration. Over-mighty nationalism, such as the expansionist aggression of Hitler's Germany, was seen as the primary threat to world peace. International solidarity to protect smaller states unable to mount an independent defense against such a threat was therefore the principal aim. The inviolability of the sovereignty of the state, set out in Article 2, was the working premise and the essential building block of the UN system. Laid on top of the pragmatic purpose of defending nation-states from one another's aggrandizing behavior was the belief that the principles governing such a 'World Organization' would enable it to belong on, and exemplify, a higher moral plane than the mere nation-states who made up its membership.[4]

This moral cause is reflected in the Charter's language. The preamble is a model of noble aspirations. It famously begins: 'We the peoples of the United Nations determined to save succeeding generations from the scourge of war, which twice in our lifetime has brought untold sorrow to mankind ...' and goes on to assert faith in fundamental human rights, equal rights of men and women, of nations large and small, and the determination 'to promote social progress and better standards of life in larger freedom.' To these ends, international peace and security was to be maintained by the establishment of principles, methods and institutions so that armed force – recruited from the major powers – would not be used except in the common interest, and the 'economic and social improvement of all peoples' would be advanced.

However, the aspirational language was essentially a mask. What was actually being set up was no new world order, but a framework in which international action could be pursued while the nations continued, albeit with more co-operation, along their respective paths. No independent power was granted to the new world body: power resided in the new institutions where it resided in the world – then with the Big Five, or more accurately, with the US, the USSR and Britain, and it will always ultimately reside where power resides in the world. This is an immutable fact of UN life.

Through the new mechanisms, the Big Powers would still be able to boss smaller states about, but small states would not be able to boss them. And if equality among nations was a mirage, 'We the peoples …' was a delusion. Membership of the UN was limited to states parties; and without the Axis powers, or any of the yet-to-be-decolonized British, French, Dutch or Portuguese territories, that meant 51 eligible candidates, compared to today's total of 192, including those spurned on wartime grounds at San Francisco. There were to be some opportunities for 'we the peoples …' to observe or influence UN activities, but no-one other than representatives of governments and designated officials could then, or can now, take part in formal proceedings.

Despite what a leading US historian of the UN, Thomas Franck, describes as 'cosmic over-selling' of the Charter to the public in the US, none of the negotiators involved at the time imagined that they were acting as midwives to a prototype world government of immaculate credentials – a public over-expectation that has dogged the UN down the years. Indeed, the myth still survives, and not just among extremist liberal US groups: witness the misleading title of the English edition of a contemporary book by the historian Paul Kennedy: *The Parliament of Man: the United Nations and the Quest for World Government*. The UN is decidedly not a Parliament (let alone of 'man'), and it is not, nor has ever been, trying to rule the world. Rather, the founders were creating a setting in which the difficult, painful, complex, and frustrating business of multilateral diplomacy could be pursued on an ongoing basis, rather than engaged in as an occasional one-off show at Dumbarton Oaks, San Francisco, or somewhere else that could afford to host an international circus.

So at the very outset of the new international era in which these 'United Nations' were to play a part, there were very different expectations among informed statesmen and diplomats, as compared to citizens and well-wishers, concerning what the bodies replacing those of the defunct League could realistically achieve. If the more mundane, mechanistic view had been uppermost, much of the subsequent hue and cry about the failures of 'the UN' might have been more muted. But the way the unanimity at San Francisco was communicated to a febrile world at the glorious moment when the war was finally drawing to an end raised anticipations of quite another order.

The subsequent story of the UN system reflects this dichotomy of expectations. Idealists and international activists, including those on the payroll of one or other of its member organizations, want the different bodies to have identities of their own and to stand above the machinations of their most influential governmental contributors, and are constantly disappointed by the limitations of multi-state oversight, financial dependency on state largesse, and lack of corporate executive power. By contrast, diplomats who see the UN as a club of nation-states, in which issues of importance to all or several of its members can be pursued in a more-or-less neutral environment, and whose decisions are bound to suffer from all the compromises required by consensual agreement, are very resistant to UN bodies developing a life and power of their own – unless the exercise of that power supports what they want to do. How to exercise power on behalf of an essentially powerless structure is a contradiction at the heart of all UN affairs.

The Charter bodies

When people refer to 'the United Nations', intentionally or otherwise they are usually only referring to the three best-known institutions set up by the Charter: the two arenas in which the UN's main political and diplomatic activity take place, the General Assembly and the Security Council, where decision-making is by member states; and the UN Secretariat, the bureaucratic apparatus staffed by international civil servants that services them (see box, 'UN staffing'). All member states take part on an equal footing in the General Assembly, representing the principle of equality among sovereign powers. This has one main annual session, attended during its first two weeks by Heads of State or their foreign secretaries, but business continues year-round in committees and sub-committees attended by staff of embassies to the UN. The Security Council, where real power resides, has 15 seats. Five are occupied by the ambassadors of the 'permanent members' armed with their vetoes; ten others rotate between the rest of the member states and occupants are replaced periodically by vote.

The Secretariat, headed by the Secretary-General, also services two other bodies whose powers and workings were set out in the Charter: the Trusteeship Council (whose task was to manage certain dependent territories from which the colonial power had withdrawn, and supervise their transition to self-rule); and the Economic and Social Council (ECOSOC) charged with pursuit of economic and social issues at the international level. Since 1956, these bodies have all resided in the specially built UN Headquarters, overlooking the East River in New York, on land donated by the industrialist John D Rockefeller and designated

UN staffing

The UN Secretariat and the funds, programs and specialized agencies in close relationship with it use a common system for staffing, salaries, allowances and benefits. In early 2008, 52,000 people were hired on these terms.

Different conditions apply to those in international professional (IP), and director (D) posts and above (Assistant and Under SG), and those hired locally; the latter are 'general service' (GS) and their status is lower, as are their emoluments (because employed in their home countries). The international service is like any diplomatic cadre, and pay scales are commensurate with the US foreign service. Under D level, promotion within any UN organization depends on job performance and staff review. There are competitive exams for junior professional entry.

Contrary to widespread myth, UN staff are not hugely overpaid. Compared to international NGOs they do better; but not to industrialized countries' civil service scales (especially when the US dollar is low: this is what the system is tied to). Internationals from poor developing countries may earn fabulous sums compared to their own civil service, but they have to live in the economy they are posted into. Salaries for GS staff are set at rates assessed in the locality for equivalent jobs.

Some UN bodies employ national (N) professionals – IPs cannot work in their own country. This is to avoid a situation where the staff member experiences any conflict of interest or pressure from their government. The N category was subsequently invented so that local knowledge and experience would not be denied to UN development co-operation programs. Their pay scales are set locally too.

International salaries are not tax-free. UN staff pay 'staff assessment', a substantial UN internal tax. This is mainly used to pay the tax bill of US employees; the US does not exempt their international civil service citizens from domestic taxation, but they cannot have different terms of employment so the UN repays them.

Where the system falls down is that recruitment is slow and cumbersome, and there does have to be a spread of nationalities. Some weak candidates get in, and some good ones from English-speaking countries (including in South Asia) do not because their nationalities are over-represented.

In some, but not all, UN organizations, staff gain permanent contracts after four years, and it is very difficult to fire poor performers. The nationality card is used by some countries to leverage their people into the system, especially into top layers. That there is dead wood, and some holders of sinecures who do little, is incontestable. ◼

Sources: www.un.org/Depts/OHRM/salaries_allowances/common.htm; www.un.org/Depts/OHRM/examin/exam.htm

international territory – to the irritation of some New Yorkers who convince themselves that UN diplomats and civil servants cost their city more in unpaid taxes and parking tickets than the income they bring in. A sixth body, the International Court of Justice or World Court, assumed from an identical predecessor in The Hague the task of adjudicating disputes brought to it by member states.

These six organizations are sometimes known as the 'principal organs' – a misnomer, like so much UN vocabulary. The Trusteeship Council has long been a relic; the World Court – not to be confused with the International Criminal Court established in 2002 – was hardly used for many decades; and ECOSOC with its many committees and expert bodies has never been a driving force in one of the most important areas of UN activity in the post-colonial world: international co-operation for economic and social development. The General Assembly, Security Council and the Secretariat do have a claim to represent the *crème de la crème* of the United Nations system, given the importance attached to the task of promoting international peace and security. However, this does not mean that the UN Secretariat is the supervisor and controller of the rest of the system, commanding power over all organizations with 'UN' in their title.

The United Nations does not have a monolithic structure. All significant member organizations in the UN family have their own statutes, mandates, administrations, governing bodies and staff; and their own funding arrangements. This structurally decentralized character is deliberate: if political problems jam up the international security apparatus, the rest of the organizations can avoid contamination and carry on regardless. There is, broadly speaking, a common system of administrative practice and procedure (purchasing, contracts, terms of employment and staff benefits), and the governing boards of the organizations are all composed – usually exclusively – of representatives of member states. But that is all. One of the system's most important features is that it is a loose network, with lines of authority and statutory linkages between organizations, but considerable room for organizational action. Whatever the central and superior role of the political machinery, it is only that. The General Assembly and Security Council are not the UN *per se*, nor does the Secretariat servicing them 'head' the bureaucracy except by having within it the office of the most senior UN official. It is essential to understand this, as it makes any assessment of the United Nations *as a whole* impossible.

The Secretary-General

Nowhere is the ambiguity of powerful and powerless more explicit than in the role of the Secretary-General (SG). This person – so far always a male – is both the world's diplomat-in-chief and the lackey of the Security Council and General Assembly. He has to steer a course – eloquently described by one Secretary-General – between the vanity of wishful thinking and aggrandizement, and the constriction of self-effacement and narrow self-limitation to the Charter terms.[5] He cannot afford – as several SGs have learnt to their cost – to upset the most powerful members, which in today's world means the US, but used to mean both the US and the USSR. He is also commander-in-chief of around

UN Secretaries-General

Trygve Lie (Norway)	1946-1952
Dag Hammarskjöld (Sweden)	1953-1961
U Thant (Burma)	1961-1971
Kurt Waldheim (Austria)	1972-1981
Javier Pérez de Cuéllar (Peru)	1982-1991
Boutros Boutros-Ghali (Egypt)	1992-1996
Kofi Annan (Ghana)	1997-2006
Ban Ki Moon (South Korea)	2007-

The SG and top appointments

As well as being able to appoint people to top jobs in the Secretariat, the SG is also responsible for appointing the heads of major Funds and Programs. Normally, he follows the advice of the organization's governing council or Executive Board. In the case of UNDP and UNICEF, the successful candidate has always been American, and these posts are regarded informally as a US preserve. The Nordics, who give more to UNICEF than the US, have tried to break the pattern, unsuccessfully so far. First they have to put forward a really good candidate; and, more problematically, an SG who is feeling generally beleaguered by the US administration will not needlessly antagonize it by rejecting their person. The heads of the Specialized Agencies are elected by their own governing bodies, who are responsible for some dreadful choices (see chapters 2 and 4). However much one might prefer an open competition for top UN jobs, this would require that the SG and the member states in governing bodies relinquish power over these appointments – not a likely scenario. ∎

80,000 peacekeepers. In these, as in all the tasks the member states (in their wisdom and sometimes delinquency) land upon him, the SG and his staff are also dependent upon them for the resources and legitimacy to carry them out. Contributors are notoriously stingy with funds and often refuse to pay up, and the legitimacy they confer is often hedged about with impracticable caveats and subject to withdrawal.

As the executive head of the UN Secretariat, the SG is chief of the international civil service, and this role of international bureaucrat *extraordinaire* within his Secretariat domain (and indirectly in some of the rest of the system, see box 'The SG and top appointments') is the only area of real power that he has; other power is notional and depends on the fluctuating stature of the UN as a moral and consensual force. The reality that his role was without independent clout compared to other 'world leaders' was not readily accepted by one SG with imperialist tendencies, Boutros Boutros-Ghali (1992-96). By contrast, Kurt Waldheim (1972-81), glided happily into the position, so much the cautious civil servant determined not to upset the big powers that he was described as behaving like 'a head waiter in a restaurant'.[6] U Thant (1961-71), courageous and high principled, was bawled out by US Secretary of State Dean Rusk for daring to remonstrate over the war in Vietnam: 'Who do you think you are, a country?'[7] How to balance being a 'Secretary' and a 'General' is a tension facing every occupant of the office. The first SG, Trygve Lie, greeted his successor with the words: 'You are about to enter the most impossible job on this earth.'[8]

A vague job description

The Charter is vague about the Secretary-General's responsibilities, but is clear that the office and all those serving in UN positions are to be independent from pressures exerted by member-states and are answerable only to the UN itself. This principle was sorely tried during the McCarthy witch-hunt for closet US communists; Trygve Lie betrayed it by allowing the FBI to set up an office within the UN building (later dismantled) to vet all Americans on the staff – a blot on the UN escutcheon which took years to erase. The notion of personal neutrality – of the SG or other officials – was never given credence by the USSR, which fell out with both Lie and his successor, Dag Hammarskjöld (1953-61).

The Charter also gave the SG a wide discretion to bring to the attention of the Security Council 'any matter which in his opinion may threaten the maintenance of international peace and security' (Article 99). On this basis, successive Secretaries-General – especially Hammarskjöld, and the post-Cold War office-holders Boutros-Ghali and Kofi Annan (1997-2006) – managed (erratically) to carve out independent space for undertaking pro-active initiatives. Precedent, originally set by Lie, who confounded the Security Council in its early days by providing his unsolicited opinion on a particular international crisis, has been consolidated over time; it is underwritten by the moral force carried by the SG as a kind of secular pope (without the Vatican's Swiss Guard or treasure trove). But if he crosses the constantly shifting line laid down by the strongest member(s), his position may be rendered untenable.

The selection of the SG takes place in the Security Council, more or less in secret, and candidates may be vetoed by the five permanent members. As a result, the candidate selected is the one exciting no major objections, from whatever region is agreed to deserve 'next turn' – a potential recipe for mediocrity. The two Secretaries-General to gain international superstar status and do most for the UN's reputation – Hammarskjöld and Annan – would never have been chosen if this possibility had been foreseen. Secretaries-General have to find ways of circumventing the knee-jerk 'no' tendencies to groundbreaking proposals they bring to the Security Council or General Assembly, and instead cajoling them to say 'yes'. The creation of peacekeeping at the Suez crisis in 1956, and its expansion into peace-building under Javier Pérez de Cuéllar (1982-91) and Boutros-Ghali, are appropriate examples.

Early evolution

The operations of many of the non-political organs of the UN system were not addressed in the Charter because existing international bodies were simply co-opted into the new framework. One of these was the UN Relief and Rehabilitation Administration (UNRRA), set up in 1943 to help countries liberated by Allied armies. This very first 'UN' organization undertook what much later became an important role: the delivery of humanitarian assistance on a major scale to people devastated by war and disaster.

After 1946, the Truman Administration refused any longer to support post-war reconstruction in countries under Soviet control. UNRRA's role was assumed by the US Marshall Plan for western Europe only, and its remaining assets handed over to a new UN international emergency fund mandated to help only children, UNICEF.[9] This temporary organization was the first UN body created by the General Assembly to meet special circumstances and never subsequently wound up. Due to one or more countries' vested interests (in this case Pakistan), almost all UN organizations set up to deal with a particular crisis or issue of contemporary concern have proved very difficult to kill. For example, the UN body created to monitor the armistice agreements between the new state of Israel and its neighbors in 1948 still operates out of Jerusalem today.

Post-war humanitarian work under the 'neutral' UN was therefore sidelined by the Marshall Plan, a clear indication that strategic interests still governed the conduct of international relations, even in the humanitarian context. Sixty years on, that situation has radically changed: UN bodies, some with temporary mandates for particular post-war or post-disaster crises, are now universally regarded as the primary locus of international humanitarian endeavor; many member organizations of the UN system (as well as NGOs) take part; and there is a special Office for the Co-ordination of Humanitarian Affairs (OCHA) in the UN Secretariat, headed by its own Under-Secretary-General. In the post-1945 world, an important exception in the humanitarian context was made for aid to, and resettlement of, refugees: the International Refugee Organization began work in Geneva, where it was later transformed into the UN High Commissioner for Refugees (UNHCR). In 1961, the delivery of food aid was entrusted to a new multilateral UN body, the World Food Programme* (WFP).

* Although this book generally adopts US spelling, the titles of UN organizations are rendered as they themselves spell them.

Great expectations

Independent or separate UN bodies

The 'specialized agencies' earlier set up under the League of Nations either resumed their functions, or were reconstituted with some modifications. Some of these were longstanding – the International Telecommunications Union (1868) and the Universal Postal Union (1878), for example, but their assimilation under the UN umbrella was essentially *pro forma*. This is also the case for bodies such as the World Meteorological Organization, the International Maritime Organization and many others. Of the four main specialized agencies, the International Labour Organization (ILO) was the oldest (1919); its tripartite structure – the governing body being made up of governments, employers, and trades unions in equal proportion – is unique in the system. The Food and Agriculture Organization (FAO) restarted work from its predecessor in late 1945; the World Health Organization (WHO) was re-established in 1946; the UN Educational, Scientific and Cultural Organization (UNESCO) likewise.

These bodies have their own funding sources (see box, 'Funding the UN'), are independent of the UN Secretariat and have entirely separate and autonomous governing structures, although their heads confer in a special committee (the Chief Executives Board) chaired by the Secretary-General. The headquarters of these organizations were distributed around Europe in recognition of the European contribution to the spirit of internationalism. Another set of independent organizations nesting misleadingly in the UN's family tree are the Bretton Woods institutions, set up in July 1944 to regulate international monetary and financial arrangements. The two key bodies were the International Bank for Reconstruction and Development (IBRD) to provide loans on concessionary rates, now absorbed into the expanded group of organizations better known as the World Bank; and

Funding the UN

The budget for the UN proper (the Secretariat and its programs) is approved by the General Assembly for two-year periods. The most recent budget for which information is readily available was US$3.16 billion for 2004-05. Member countries owe dues according to assessments based on their capacity to pay, which is determined by their gross national incomes and adjusted to take other factors into account.

The financing situation of the UN is precarious because member states – notably the US, the largest contributor, providing around 22 per cent – sometimes withhold their dues or fail to pay on time. To keep going, the UN solicits voluntary contributions from other members, borrows from a Working Capital Fund, or from separate peacekeeping budgets. The budget for 16 peacekeeping operations for 2006-07 was around US$5 billion.

UN Funds and Programs are each financed separately, by voluntary contributions from member states; this makes their resources vulnerable to fluctuations in international esteem. UNICEF also has 37 national committees which raise funds from the public, providing a third of its income; financial pressures have recently encouraged other UN organizations to collect money from non-government sources. Examples of budgetary size: UNDP 2006-07 (also covering subsidiary programs such as UNIFEM): US$9.2 billion; UNHCR 2007: US$1.5 billion; UNICEF 2008-09 (anticipated): US$6.7 billion.

The Specialized Agencies receive funds from member states on an assessment basis, in a way similar to the UN Secretariat, and also seek additional voluntary contributions. WHO's proposed budget for biennium 2006-07 was US$3.2 billion; UNESCO's regular (assessed) budget for 2006-2007 was US$610 million. Budgetary information can be found (sometimes with difficulty) on the relevant organizational websites.

In terms of what the whole UN system does, the costs are not exorbitant. For comparison, the annual budget of the Greater London Authority is around US$10 billion, twice the cost of all UN peacekeeping and three times the UN Secretariat budget. ∎

Source: UN websites and Basic Facts about the United Nations, UN New York, 2003.

the International Monetary Fund (IMF). Although they are co-members of the international system and function according to similar procedures, the Bretton Woods institutions operate entirely separately from the United Nations. In the field of international development (see chapter 4), where an important role is played by multilateral assistance programs, there has often been competition between UN and Bretton Woods institutions – which the latter normally win.

Great expectations

A bewildering proliferation of UN Commissions and bodies such as Funds, Offices, Institutes and a University, gradually emerged under the spreading UN canopy over the following decades. Bodies such as the UN Development Programme (UNDP), the UN Population Fund (UNFPA) and the UN Environment Programme (UNEP) nominally operate under the UN Secretariat umbrella, and some have close co-operative arrangements. But they have essentially charted their own paths and developed their own identities, reporting annually to General Assembly committees more as a formality than to seek genuine direction. Their scope and size depends largely on whether they are able to raise funds effectively. The nature of some of these organizations will become clearer during subsequent chapters.

What is important to note here is that, despite the spanner thrown in the works by the division of the world into two superpower blocs from 1946 to 1989, the framework set up by the Charter proved sufficiently elastic to allow the development of the UN system to go ahead. New institutions to address different issues or serve different regions have been set up under the broad church of ECOSOC, or have adopted a more or less independent existence by resolution of the General Assembly. Rather than representing a cornucopia of extravagance and red tape, the way this has come about illustrates the fundamental flexibility of the system, as well as the acceptance by its hugely expanded membership that issues placed on the international agenda by common acclaim – from the situation of indigenous peoples to the sharing of cross-boundary water resources, from climate change to the elaboration of women's rights – can and should find appropriate homes within the labyrinth of UN machinery.

Whether the machinery invariably performs well is another matter. And whether some institutions have outlived their usefulness is yet another. The responsibility for creating these bodies, and for their oversight and would-be dissolution, rests with the member states – not with the machinery itself. And if they cannot reach consensus about streamlining the system then the process becomes stymied. Limited programs of reform have been achieved, but have required Herculean efforts of diplomacy (see chapter 7).

A bewildering complexity

Trying to fathom how the UN system works is mind-bendingly difficult. There are in effect two overlapping anarchies: one created by the governance of all UN organizations by co-equal UN member states elected to their executive boards or governing councils; and another created by the constellation of UN organizations, some of which have similar mandates and seem to be constantly vying for resources and ascendancy. In order to try to explain itself, the UN puts out an organogram (see pages 30-31). But this implies a far greater degree of tidiness and neater lines of authority than actually exist; and at the same time gives no clear sense of what the system does or how its member bodies relate to one another, let alone their relative size or scope.

Shirley Hazzard, writing in 1973, stated that at no time had UN dignitaries or world leaders begun to explain the organization effectively to the public, or point out what difficulties the UN would face and what kinds of support it needed to be effectual[10] – and she was only referring to the UN proper, not to the rest of the system. Things have changed very little – if anything, they became more confusing in the period when the end of the Cold War released the constraints supposedly inhibiting the system's workings. Rarely even do governments themselves possess more than a superficial understanding of 'their' United Nations organization; the numbers of diplomats and

The United Nations System

Principal organs

Trusteeship Council	Security Council	General Assembly

Subsidiary Bodies

Military Staff Committee
Standing Committee and
ad hoc bodies
Peacekeeping Operations and
Missions
Counter-Terrorism Committee

International Criminal Tribunal for the
former Yugoslavia (ICTY)
International Criminal Tribunal for
Rwanda (ICTR)

Subsidiary Bodies

Main committees
Human Rights Council
Other sessional committees
Standing committees and ad
hoc bodies
Other subsidiary organs

Programmes and Funds

UNCTAD United Nations
Conference on Trade and
Development
  ITC International Trade Centre
  (UNCTAD/WTO)
UNDCP United Nations Drug
Control Programme
UNEP United Nations Environment
Programme
UNICEF United Nations Children's
Fund

UNDP United Nations Development
Programme
  UNIFEM United Nations
  Development Fund for Women
  UNV United Nations Volunteers
  UNCDF United Nations Capital
  Development Fund
UNFPA United Nations Population
Fund
UNHCR Office of the United Nations
High Commissioner for Refugees

Advisory Subsidiary Body
United Nations Peacebuilding
Commission

WFP World Food Programme
UNRWA United Nations
Relief and Works Agency
for Palestine Refugees in
the Near East
UN-HABITAT United Nations
Human Settlements
Programme

Research and Training Institutes

UNICRI United Nations Interregional
Crime and Justice Research
Institute
UNITAR United Nations Institute for
Training and Research

UNRISD United Nations Research
Institute for Social Development
UNIDIR United Nations Institute for
Disarmament Research

UN-INSTRAW United Nations
International Research
and Training Institute
for the Advancement of
Women

Other UN Entities

UNOPS United Nations Office for Project Services
UNU United Nations University

UNSSC United Nations System Staff College
UNAIDS Joint United Nations Programme
on HIV/AIDS

Other UN Trust Funds

UNFIP United Nations Fund for International Partnerships

UNDEF United Nations Democracy Fund

ARROWS: Solid lines from a Principal Organ indicate a direct reporting
relationship; dashes indicate a non-subsidiary relationship.

Economic and Social Council

Functional Commissions
Commissions on:
  Narcotic Drugs
  Crime Prevention and
    Criminal Justice
  Science and Technology for
    Development
  Sustainable Development
  Status of Women
  Population and Development
Commission for Social
  Development
Statistical Commission

Regional Commissions
Economic Commission for
  Africa (ECA)
Economic Commission for
  Europe (ECE)
Economic Commission for Latin
  America and the Caribbean
  (ECLAC)
Economic and Social
  Commission for Asia and the
  Pacific (ESCAP)
Economic and Social
  Commission for Western
  Asia (ESCWA)

Other Bodies
Permanent Forum on Indigenous
  Issues
United Nations Forum on Forests
Sessional and standing
  committees
Expert, ad hoc and related
  bodies

Related Organizations
WTO World Trade Organization
IAEA International Atomic
  Energy Agency

CTBTO Prep.Com PrepCom
  for the Nuclear Test Ban Treaty
  Organizations
OPCW Organization for the
  Prohibition of Chemical Weapons

International Court of Justice

Specialized Agencies
ILO International Labour
  Organization
FAO Food and Agriculture
  Organization of the United
  Nations
UNESCO United Nations
  Educational, Scientific and
  Cultural Organization
WHO World Health Organization

World Bank Group
  IBRD International Bank
    for Reconstruction and
    Development
  IDA International
    Development Association
  IFC International Finance
    Corporation
  MIGA Multilateral
    Investment Guarantee
    Agency
  ICSID International Centre
    for Settlement of Investment
    Disputes
IMF International Monetary
  Fund
ICAO International Civil Aviation
  Organization
IMO International Maritime
  Organization
ITU International
  Telecommunications Union
UPU Universal Postal Union
WMO World Meteorological
  Organization
WIPO World Intellectual Property
  Organization
IFAD International Fund for
  Agricultural Development
UNIDO United Nations Industrial
  Development Organization
UNWTO World Tourism
  Organization

Secretariat

Departments and Offices
OSG Office of the Secretary-
  General
OIOS Office of Internal Oversight
  Services
OLA Office of Legal Affairs
DPA Department of Political
  Affairs
UNODA Office for Disarmament
  Affairs
DPKO Department of
  Peacekeeping Operations
DFS Department of Field Support
OCHA Office for the Coordination
  of Humanitarian Affairs
DESA Department of Economic
  and Social Affairs
DGACM Department for General
  Assembly and Conference
  Management
DPI Department of Public
  Information
DM Department of Management
UN-OHRLLS Office of the High
  Representative for the
  Least Developed Countries,
  Landlocked Developing
  Countries and Small Island
  Developing States
OHCHR Office of the United
  Nations High Commissioner
  for Human Rights
UNODC United Nations Office on
  Drugs and Crime
DSS Department of Safety and
  Security

UNOG UN Office at Geneva
UNOV UN Office at Vienna
UNON UN Office at Nairobi

civil servants who fully grasp how the machinery works outside the patch on which they operate must be extraordinarily few. This *No-Nonsense Guide* unavoidably suffers from similar limitations. Its journey through UN mechanisms and their performance carries its own biases and black holes, compounded by serious restrictions of space.

This chapter has tried to set out the great difficulties confronting all of the machinery, especially of the political variety, of asserting its own course of action; and yet show respect for the farsightedness of those who knew that without such built-in restraints, it would never be used. The machinery moves forward, where it can move at all, inhibited by multiple tugs of war. Ironically, this may ultimately be one of its greatest strengths. Exploring this contradiction is a subject to return to later. For the moment we will take the main areas of activity one by one. And because it is quintessential, 'international security' is where we begin.

1 'The New Charter', *The Economist*, London, 30 June 1945. **2** *The Times*, London, 27 June 1945. **3** Thomas M Franck, *Nation against Nation: What happened to the UN dream?* Oxford University Press, New York, 1985. **4** Adam Roberts and Benedict Kingsbury (Eds), *United Nations, Divided World*, first edition 1988, second revised edition 1993, Oxford University Press. **5** Javier Pérez de Cuéllar, 'The Role of the UN Secretary-General', in Roberts and Kingsbury 1993, op cit. **6** Kenneth W Stein, *Heroic Diplomacy: Sadat, Kissinger, Carter, Begin, and the Quest for Arab-Israeli Peace*, Routledge, New York, 1999. **7** James Traub, *The Best Intentions: Kofi Annan and the UN in the Era of American Power*, Bloomsbury, London, 2006. **8** Simon Chesterman (Ed), *Secretary or General? The UN Secretary-General in world politics*, Cambridge University Press, 2007. **9** Maggie Black, *The Children and the Nations*, UNICEF, 1986; revised edition with Macmillan, Australia, 1987. **10** Shirley Hazzard, *Defeat of an Ideal*, Macmillan, London, 1973.

2 Ending the scourge of war

The havoc wreaked in so many countries by the Second World War and the desire to prevent this ever happening again was the impetus behind the creation of the UN. Its subsequent failure to step in and prevent wars or stop them in their tracks has been the principal complaint leveled at the organization down the years. In fact, the inherent limitations stemming from its nature as a collective forum for member states make this task immensely difficult, independently of the stand-off between the superpowers which imposed paralysis from 1946 until 1989. Nonetheless, the UN did manage to carve out a political role in promoting international security. Since the Cold War ended, that role has expanded.

KEEPING THE PEACE was overwhelmingly the task for which the United Nations was created. The idea of 'collective security' underlay peace enforcement by the new institutions. The proposition at its simplest was that all member countries would join in common 'UN' action against any country threatening the security of another state.[1] As we saw in chapter 1, maintaining the integrity of the nation-state, and the corollary, non-intervention in its domestic affairs, were the bedrock of the new international system. The key provisions on meeting aggression, in Chapter VII of the UN Charter, supposedly contain the 'teeth' that the covenant of the League of Nations had lacked. They include diplomacy and sanctions, leading up to military action by forces lent for the purpose by member states.

Within two days of the Security Council's inaugural ceremony in January 1946, the widening cracks between East and West and their impact on the potential for UN action were revealed. The first threat to 'the peace' brought before the Council concerned Iran – interestingly, given today's preoccupations. The issue was the removal of wartime Russian troops still stationed there, who – like US and UK contingents – were supposed to go home.[2] After remonstrations, the USSR finally agreed to withdraw them.

The Soviet Union stated openly that it did not believe in genuine co-operation between the capitalist and communist worlds, and treated successive Secretaries-General and UN bodies with such distrust that it seems in retrospect a miracle that the UN survived its early years. Instead, the new forum was treated as a theater for acting out superpower opposition. This had a buffering effect, helping protagonists work through confrontations and adding something behind the scenes to bilateral prevention of armed attack (including during the Cuban missile crisis). But the gridlock was always projected negatively. The UN was covered by news media much more prominently in the 1950s and 1960s than it is now. The most notorious photo in UN history, flashed by newswires around the world, was of President Nikita Khruschev in October 1960, pounding his shoe on the desk in front of him in protest against anti-Soviet statements in the General Assembly.

In 1948, the USSR withdrew its co-operation from the Security Council over the US-led refusal to admit Communist China to UN membership in place of the Nationalists exiled in Taiwan. As a result, Russian delegates were not present at the debates in 1950 on the North Korean invasion of South Korea. When they resumed their seat, the matter was referred to the General Assembly, where the US was sure of a majority in its favor. Therefore the USSR failed to apply their veto and prevent 'the UN' – effectively the US with allied support – going to war in South Korea's defense.[3] Until the 1991 Gulf War, Korea was the only UN-sanctioned military campaign undertaken to 'enforce peace': a tautological phrase often used in UN parlance, meaning 'resist aggression'. The USSR learnt its lesson, and the mistake of non-cooperation was never repeated.

Thus, by a reactive retreat into engagement, the Soviet Union – despite all its reservations about Western domination of the UN – grudgingly joined in. It used the arena to pursue a proxy conflict with the West in all sorts of forums, vetoing and grandstanding on behalf of satellites and strategic friends (Vietnam included). This behavior also helped to anchor the US in the UN orbit, even though down the years it became increasingly less enchanted with the body that, originally, it had proprietarily thought of as 'its own'.

Flashpoint Middle East

At the beginning of its life, the situation in Palestine seemed like the only political problem that the UN was positioned to resolve. Free of Soviet-US tension, the Middle East conflict was powered by weaker antagonists: the Jews, the Arabs, and the declining British Empire.

The UN midwifed the birth of the Jewish state in 1948, and Arab-Israeli hatred occupied much subsequent UN time and effort. But, as more countries joined, the UN's intentions became suspect, especially to the Israelis. The most significant Security Council action concerning the Middle East was the passage of Resolution 242 in 1967, which demanded a withdrawal of Israeli forces from territories occupied during the Six-Day War, in return for respecting the integrity and sovereignty of every state in the region – including Israel. This resolution has remained the basis for negotiations, including the Israeli-Egyptian accord at Camp David in 1979. But by the time the Oslo accords were brokered between Israel and the Palestinian Liberation Organization (PLO) in 1993, the UN had become a distant observer. This situation continues in the present day, with the UN merely a member rather than leader of the 'quartet' – the US, Russia, Europe and the UN – trying to find a way out of the current morass.

The Suez crisis in 1956 – widely regarded by historians as the moment at which the imperialist era came to an end – was also a high point for the UN. The British and French, in secret collusion with Israel, launched an attack on Egypt intended to recover control over the Suez Canal, recently nationalized by President Nasser. The two colonial powers were roundly condemned, most importantly by the US – which put the matter in the UN's lap. The UN's political machinery under the aegis of Dag Hammarskjöld came into its own. This was the most important occasion up to that time on which the Secretary-General managed to assert, by astute diplomacy, the UN's moral ascendancy in smoothing extremely troubled international waters.

Since the Security Council was blocked by Anglo-French vetoes, resolution was again shifted into the General Assembly, which authorized the first ever UN peacekeeping force, the United Nations Emergency Force in Sinai (UNEF); this remained the blueprint for UN peacekeeping until the end of the Cold War. Its purpose was to replace the Anglo-French and Israeli forces then occupying the Canal zone with troops operating under UN command, enabling their withdrawal with some respect intact. The UN thus provided an escape route, and prevented the conflict deepening.

This kind of peacekeeping was not envisaged by the UN Charter. Funds had to be solicited specially from the UN's principal donors. Its creation was an inspired innovation by Hammarskjöld and his aides. The model was subsequently used – either as an interposing force, or in an observer form – with varying degrees of success in a number of conflicts during the Cold War period, in the Congo, Yemen, India-Pakistan, Cyprus (where blue-bereted UN peacekeepers have been present since 1964), and in Lebanon (1978). All these were situations where the superpowers were either not closely implicated or were not sufficiently exercised to use their vetoes in the Security Council.

More recently, the failures of UN peacekeepers – because they were too few, not empowered to shoot, or got drawn in on one side of an internal conflict – have demonstrated how powerless and ineffective such missions can be in circumstances where there is no peace to keep. This has helped to generate a new debate and new constructs for UN political activity, which we will come to later.

Decolonization

The context of international affairs is dynamic, and the UN both reflects and has to respond to new currents. In the 1960s and 1970s, the most important of these was decolonization, and the arrival at independence of new states in Africa, Indo-China, the Caribbean and the Pacific. During the 1950s, the 'wind of change' – a phrase immortalized by Harold Macmillan – blew down the African continent in stormy gusts, and where in the previous century European powers had scrambled to gain territories, they now scrambled to give them up.

At the UN, Hammarskjöld raised high the flag of the self-determination of peoples. The trusteeship division under Ralph Bunche provided a brokerage service for the elaboration of constitutions and handover arrangements. The watershed year was 1960: 14 former French colonies and three others (Congo, Somalia and Nigeria) became independent and joined the UN. Within a few years, most of the rest followed suit. Concern over recalcitrants, especially where racism stood in the way of democracy in southern Africa, haunted deliberations at the UN for many years to come.

Ending the scourge of war

The most immediate impact on the UN was the fracturing in some of these patched-together countries, and the attempt in the Congo to deploy peacekeepers to glue it back together. Dag Hammarskjöld lost his life when his plane crashed in Zambia in 1961 en route to negotiations between the antagonists. The experience in the Congo, in which, eventually, UN forces took action to end the secession of Katanga province – a breach of the non-intervention principle – caused huge angst, and antagonized the USSR, especially against Hammarskjöld. As a result, there was a collective feeling of 'never again'. UN military peacekeepers were not again sent to Africa until 1992.

However, the UN was embroiled in humanitarian activity in the Nigerian civil war (1968-71) and in many other emergencies (covered in chapter 3). Non-military UN personnel took a major role in the coming to independence of Namibia in 1990 following its long colonial administration by South Africa. But from 1964 to 1989, although active in the context of apartheid and the illegal white regime in Southern Rhodesia (ending with Zimbabwe's independence in 1980), the UN's political machinery stayed away from direct involvement in African wars. Most had to do with the break-up of fragile states, and the principle of sovereignty and the interdict on interfering in internal affairs inhibited UN action. Besides, many wars – in the Horn of Africa between Ethiopia and Somalia, for instance, and in Angola and Mozambique – were abetted on their opposite sides by the superpowers, and international action was effectively paralyzed. Western security alliances with apartheid South Africa further muddied the waters.

Growth in membership
The most important impact of decolonization on the UN was the rapid growth in membership. By 1961, the number of member states had grown from 51 to 100;

by 1985, to 159; by 1993, to 184; and the grand total today is 192.[4] This is entirely a product of the collapse of empires and associated break-ups; very few countries have amalgamated in this time (Germany being a notable exception).

When decolonization began, the US and USSR were competing for allegiance among the crowd of newborn and adolescent countries. In 1955, Presidents Nehru of India, Sukarno of Indonesia, Nasser of Egypt, Tito of Yugoslavia and Nkrumah of Ghana launched the Non-Aligned Movement and declared their intention to answer to neither of the superpowers. At the United Nations, the 'emerging nations' became known as the Group of 77. No longer could the US and its allies gain an automatic majority in the General Assembly.

Instead, the Group of 77 used the UN as a platform to articulate their international aspirations – against neo-colonialism, racism and other forms of subordination or discrimination. Acting together, they could block US-led initiatives. For example, Communist China finally took up its UN seat in 1971 because the US could no longer sufficiently control voting in the General Assembly so as to keep it out. The growth in UN membership thus had an important influence on the functioning of the UN's political apparatus. This depends on unity between member states to function well, and the larger and more diverse the membership, the more elusive such unity is likely to be.

The other impact of decolonization was to energize those parts of the UN whose purpose was to support the other main area of activity anticipated by the founders: 'the economic and social front where victory means freedom from want'.[5] Idealistic as this sounded, the wider social advance that much of the UN network existed to support could not remain free of political taint. In 1961, when US President John Kennedy launched the UN's first 'Development Decade', he openly reinforced the politicization of this next round of UN endeavor: aid from Western sources for 'developing' countries was, in part, a tool for winning allegiance in the ongoing capitalist-communist battle.

The attack on the UN

The influx of new members established the UN as the world's first truly universal organization.[6] UN recognition became *the* seal of international approval conferring legitimacy on a country's claim to statehood, and membership was a much sought-after prize. But the flexing of new members' international muscles led in directions inimical to the US, in many peripheral bodies and especially in the General Assembly, which they could now dominate by tyranny of numbers.

In the 1970s, the Group of 77 swelled to over 100 and became an organized bloc. They adopted an anti-imperialist rhetoric that, on a crude interpretation – and, at the time, interpretations tended to be crude – labeled them as quislings of international socialism and its assault on 'larger freedom'. In an atmosphere reminiscent of McCarthyism, the flamboyant Daniel Patrick Moynihan, US Ambassador to the UN from 1975-6, saw in the unlikely circumstances of the Third Committee of the General Assembly on Social, Humanitarian and Cultural Affairs, a conspiracy of totalitarians determined to undermine democratic values.[7] At this time, the US was heavily bruised by the debacle of the war in Vietnam, and allergic to ideological rhetoric disparaging the West.

Algeria's 1975 campaign to introduce anti-Zionist language into any and every UN recommendation – first up was the declaration on women's rights from the UN Women's Conference in Mexico – marked the nadir of these activities. A resolution that 'Zionism is racism' made its way through the Third Committee into the General Assembly itself, and as far as Moynihan was concerned, sounded the death-knell of the UN as a credible forum. Other observers, including the UK Ambassador Sir Ivor Richard, felt that Moynihan's posturing helped lose the day, and that a UN resolution so palpably ridiculous did not much matter.[8] That it was championed by such abusers of human rights as President Idi Amin of Uganda, whose anti-Zionist attack in the 1975 General Assembly was given an ovation, increased its absurdity. The then Secretary-General, Kurt Waldheim of Austria – whose hidden background as an army officer associated with Nazi atrocities was not exposed until later – did not succeed behind the scenes in getting the resolution quashed.

No new international order

This profusion of rhetoric followed the crisis provoked by the OPEC cartel in 1973, whereby oil-producing developing countries hiked prices and held consumers to ransom. For a while, it seemed as if the poorer countries would succeed via the UN in asserting political influence as a bloc by using their leverage over commodities. Sympathizers with the developing world regarded the key contemporary international mission as tackling the gross inequality between the industrialized 'North' and the impoverished 'South'. At the UN, this position was championed by the Argentinean economist Raúl Prebisch, Secretary-General of the UN Conference on Trade and Development (UNCTAD) (see chapter 4).

In 1974, a UN Special Session endorsed a proposal for a New International Economic Order (NIEO) to give the South more clout in international markets and monetary systems. The NIEO was anathema to the US, which began to disparage the UN on every conceivable front – aided by critics of the Moynihan stamp. It was at this time that venomous stories about the UN's squandering of resources, bloated bureaucracy, and general uselessness began to take hold in the popular mind, especially in the US. Waldheim wrung his hands and complained of the UN's limitations – but his ineffectuality quite endeared him to those who would have liked the UN to fall into the East River and simply disappear. The US began to withhold its dues: why should it pay its assigned 25 per cent of the regular budget to support this antithetical body? Member states who together paid a tiny proportion of the UN's budget, and lacked commitment to democracy and human rights, were dominating important organs. This remains the critical argument over UN power balances today.

The worst of times

The late 1970s and early 1980s can be seen as the worst period in UN history. The Heritage Foundation, advisors to the Reagan Administration, published a study in 1982 concluding: 'A world without the UN would be a better world'.[9] In a preface to a series of lectures delivered for the UN's 40th birthday in 1985, Sridath Ramphal, Commonwealth Secretary General, wrote: 'The paradox – and the tragedy – of recent times is that, even as the need for a multilateral approach to global problems has become more manifest, support for internationalism has weakened – eroded by some of the strongest nations who have in the past acknowledged their obligation of leadership. This is most true of the US, whose recent behavior has served actually to weaken the structures of multilateralism, including the UN itself.'[10] Ramphal later failed in his candidacy for the top UN post.

The most conspicuous action of antipathy towards the UN network at this time – apart from efforts to starve large parts of the system of funds – was the withdrawal by the US and UK from the UN Educational, Scientific and Cultural Organization (UNESCO). Throughout the system, there had been an inflow into UN governance bodies from the new member states, and in UNESCO's case, the corresponding politicization was compounded by criticism of its Senegalese Director-General Amadou-Mahtar M'Bow. Backed by a majority on the UNESCO board, M'Bow was able to impose a regime based on personal patronage wholly inappropriate in an international – or any – organization. UNESCO's proposed New International Information Order, chiming with the NIEO and reducing the 'free' Western media's control over international information flows, was a proposal too far. The Reagan and Thatcher administrations departed in 1984, taking their funds with them. M'Bow was eventually forced out in 1987. Mikhail Gorbachev was seeking co-operation with the West, and so the Eastern bloc withdrew support from M'Bow. Thus wider political change – the coming end of the Cold War – helped to reduce the Southern ascendancy based on membership numbers in the operations of the UN.

Throughout the early 1980s, the influence of the South, and of the UN itself, as forces in international affairs were beaten into retreat. The 1973 OPEC oil cartel was the only common show of unity the Third World managed to muster that seriously threatened the interests of the industrialized world. Similar attempts were blocked by the West once the risk was understood. When this moment of power ended, any prospect of imposing on the world any new 'order' that would substantially redistribute the levers of power was lost. For many internationalists, this was not a joyful conquest over socialist and totalitarian crazies, but a victory for Western capitalists determined to sustain a profoundly unequal world to suit themselves. In retrospect, it can be seen as an indication that the world had changed so much since 1945 and 1960, and with it the UN structures representing the political globe in microcosm, that axes such as North and South, capitalist and communist, industrialized and developing, no longer represented defining contours of international affairs. East-West was not the only axis on the wane.

In the 1970s and 1980s, the rising price of oil produced a body of super-wealthy states in the previously impoverished desert autocracies of Arabia. This effectively began the sundering of the South. Nations with huge natural resources, booming economies, investment potential, growing consumer markets and other 'developed' attributes do not belong in the same strategic or economic bucket as impoverished and unstable countries with national incomes of less than $150 a head.[11] Subsequently, there was no longer a unified 'South' nor necessarily a similarity of outlook and interests based on post-colonial status. As globalization gathered pace, new dichotomies emerged: 'tiger' economies and failed states, Samuel P Huntington's 'clash of civilizations' along cultural lines,[12] and membership versus non-membership of the nuclear weapons club. All such cross-cutting differences within the family of nations infinitely compound the problem of making any global system pursuing the overall aim of 'international security' operate well, or even at all.

New prospects and ideas

Javier Pérez de Cuéllar began his term as Secretary-General in 1982. In his first report to the General Assembly, he warned: 'The Council seems powerless... The process of peaceful settlement of disputes prescribed in the Charter is often brushed aside. Sterner measures for world peace were envisaged in Chapter VII... but the prospect of realizing such measures is now deemed almost impossible. We are perilously near to a new international anarchy.'[13] Within a few years, the USSR's shift towards co-operation with the West opened up new vistas. Pérez de Cuéllar exploited the thaw in US-Soviet relations, instituting informal meetings of the key ambassadors in the Security Council – non-meetings at which non-papers were reviewed, so that positions could be synthesized, improving Council effectiveness. His successor Boutros-Ghali refused to participate, thinking these discussions a waste of his time.

Most of the conflicts now being waged were within states not between them. The UN was in no way designed to help resolve this kind of war. But it became essential for its credibility that its machinery played a role beyond that of facilitator of humanitarian relief. In the late 1980s, it finally appeared to the US that in the new circumstances of détente with the USSR, UN-brokered peace in the civil conflicts in Central America served US interests; it similarly seemed to the USSR that a UN umbrella could usefully shelter the withdrawal of their forces from Afghanistan. The way was thus reopened for the Secretary-General personally, and the UN institutionally, to provide good offices and personnel – in blue helmets or in civvies – to help bring an end to the scourge of war.

In the early 1990s, the UN political machinery experienced a late flowering, with – once more – huge expectations surrounding its capacity to make peace around the globe. Saddam Hussein's invasion of Kuwait succeeded in uniting the Security Council behind military action under the UN flag for the Gulf War of 1991. But other conflicts involved the splintering of states, or outbreaks of violence due to internal tensions previously held in check by superpower stand-off. Still others derived from development failure, with internecine strife representing a power struggle among armed factions over wealth or the means of survival. The long list of these conflicts included Afghanistan, Somalia, Angola, Haiti, East Timor, ex-Yugoslavia and Sudan. A key difficulty for the UN was to find an acceptable basis for circumventing the inhibition about non-intervention. This had become essential for addressing these conflicts and the hideous forms of violence they contained.

The new agenda

In January 1992, the Security Council met for the first time at the level of heads of government. They declared that the end of the Cold War had 'raised hopes for a safer, more equitable and more humane world'. Secretary-General Boutros Boutros-Ghali was asked to make recommendations on how the UN's capacity for preventive diplomacy, peacemaking and peace-building could be correspondingly pepped up within the Charter framework.[14] Boutros-Ghali was intellectually gifted and the most experienced Secretary-General in foreign affairs the UN had ever had, and he saw the renewed commitment to the UN in epochal terms. His *Agenda for Peace*, outlining the measures he proposed, warned that improvements would be impossible unless the 'new spirit of commonality is propelled by the will to take the hard decisions demanded'. But the spirit of commonality between the nations is an elusive and temporary affair.

Two types of security-related action were possible under UN auspices. One included preventive diplomacy, peacemaking, and peace-building – post-conflict support for holding elections and creating an environment in which a civil administration could function. These required that the parties sought or agreed to UN involvement. Given that most states think that the UN should help solve others' internal conflicts, but rarely want it to meddle in their own (Britain's attitude to Northern Ireland being a case in point), a surprising number have used its good offices in this way. In the second type of action – sanctions or 'peace enforcement' – the consent of the Security Council, and the veto-wielding five Permanent Members, has to be given for an unwanted intervention.

The volume of peace-related activity which fell on

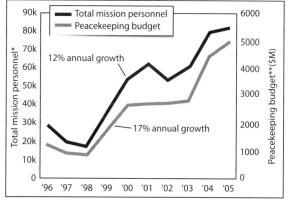

Rapid growth in UN peacekeeping

In the late 1990s and early 2000s, UN peacekeeping operations underwent massive growth, in terms of both mission personnel and budget.

Legend:
- Total mission personnel
- Peacekeeping budget

12% annual growth

17% annual growth

	'96	'97	'98	'99	'00	'01	'02	'03	'04	'05
Number of peace-keeping missions	16	14	14	16	14	12	12	11	15	15
Average personnel per mission	1816	1443	1223	2200	3917	5198	4465	5519	5315	5524

*Average two years' military & civilian staff in missions, & support account posts in HQ.
** Annual budget reflects July-to-June budget starting in that year; eg 1996 budget runs from July 1996 to June 1997,

Investing in the United Nations for a Stronger Organization Worldwide, Report of the Secretary-General, March 2006.

the UN in the 1990s was extraordinary. In 1987, the UN was involved in helping resolve 11 conflicts; by 1994, the tally was 28. Peacekeeping operations had risen from 5 to 17; military personnel, from 9,570 to 73,400; the costs, from $230 million to $3,610 million.[15] Most conflicts were internal, and many – especially in Africa – involved the collapse of state institutions, including police and judiciary, murder of functionaries and professionals, and a descent into the ungovernable condition of the 'failed state'.

The idea that a multilateral organization in no way resourced or designed for such a task could manage to sort out many extremely complex and dangerous situations – some of which governments with much larger resources had helped to create and then washed their hands of – was to expect from it things beyond its capacity both in principle and in practice. Unfortunately, expectations ran amok, and so did an element of *folie de grandeur* on the part of the UN.

Against a scaled-down set of expectations, the UN's peace-related achievements in the early post-Cold War years should be applauded. Under Pérez de Cuéllar, peacekeeping took on significant new dimensions, with forces and/or civilian personnel sent to countries such as Nicaragua (1989-91), Cambodia (1991-93) and El Salvador (1991-95)[16], to oversee elections, monitor human rights violations, disarm military units, and help restore and rebuild government institutions. These businesslike operations, completed under Boutros-Ghali, are today little remembered.

Over-reach and hubris

Disasters associated with other missions eclipsed the UN dawn. In Somalia, massive US military involvement helped save victims of a famine in 1992 caused by the country's devastation by warlords. This action, approved by the Security Council, was the first occasion on which an internal humanitarian crisis was defined as a threat to international peace, and handled under Chapter VII of the Charter.[17] Once the delivery of humanitarian assistance was secured, a smaller peacekeeping operation took over in mid-1993. But the Somali factions' intransigence, the fluidity of their alliances, and the difficulties of disarming them were not properly understood. The second operation was under the UN Secretary-General's direct control, another 'first', and one that turned out badly.

The UN forces became embroiled in fighting one

of the Somali leaders, General Mohamed Farah Aideed, thereby forfeiting any claim to impartiality. The military command was confused and contested between the UN and national contingents. Efforts to capture Aideed were futile, and several peacekeepers – and many more Somalis – lost their lives. In a notorious incident in late 1993, two Black Hawk helicopters were downed by Aideed's militia and 17 US marines were killed. Faced with domestic outcry, and without consulting Boutros-Ghali, President Clinton announced a unilateral withdrawal of US forces by March 1994. A blame game between the US Administration and the Secretary-General for the many failures of the mission poisoned relations. The UN did not have the capacity to command such an operation – one that turned out to have nothing to do with peacekeeping and itself became sucked into the armed chaos. Peace and a viable political settlement still elude Somalia 14 years on.

Somalia was a rude awakening to the practicalities of delivering on *An Agenda for Peace*, but not the only one. Simultaneously, the Balkans descended into war, and here the UN mission was mandated to deploy peacekeeping forces to police ceasefires and safeguard humanitarian relief (see chapter 3). As the civil war deepened in Bosnia-Herzegovina in 1992-93, the Security Council inched towards authorizing 'peace enforcement' measures under Chapter VII, but never with sufficient troop deployments or military clout to stop the fighting.[18] When no political solution emerged, the impossibility of maintaining UN-monitored 'safe areas' led to the 1995 Srebrenica massacre. Over Bosnia too, the US Administration fell out with Boutros-Ghali. UN resistance to the use of serious force by NATO helped prolong the war, and led to an invidious association of the UN with Bosnian-Serb aggressors. Once again, the UN demonstrated its political and military inadequacy for wartime operations, as opposed to functioning as a facilitating forum so that those states who could act effectively took political and military action to quell and disempower aggressors.

Finally, with everyone burned by Somalia, came arguably the worst Security Council and UN failure in its 50-year history: the appalling spectacle in April 1994 of UN peacekeepers in Rwanda powerless to stop the extremist Hutu genocide.

The UN had over-reached itself, and in Rwanda under-reached itself. Boutros-Ghali's determination to behave like a Head of State instead of a *haut fonctionnaire* exposed the inbuilt weaknesses of the system in their most glaring and negative light. Although it would be unfair to lay all blame at the door of the UN, whose mandate and resources in any operation depend entirely on member-state decisions and contributions, peace-related actions were often mismanaged and out of kilter with reality. Boutros-Ghali and his peacekeeping chief, Kofi Annan, should perhaps have managed to avoid taking on tasks that were under-resourced and virtually guaranteed to end badly. But how? The UN is the depository of last resort for intransigent international problems, and the Secretariat cannot refuse to carry out the demands – unrealistic though they may be – of the Security Council, especially when human suffering is screaming for a response.

If the powerful members, notably the US, are detached and uninterested, as they were at the time of the Rwanda massacres, and unwilling to commit resources or troops, the UN is helpless. After the debacle in Somalia, the US declared itself unwilling to participate in UN peacekeeping or peace enforcement actions unless they were in its national interest. Russia and China have similarly chosen to inhibit UN effectiveness to suit their pocketbooks and political interests over the conflict in Darfur.

In jeopardy once more

Purely at US insistence, in 1997 Boutros-Ghali was not granted a second term, instead being replaced by Kofi Annan. The only Secretary-General to be appointed from within the system, Annan was every inch the self-effacing civil servant that Boutros-Ghali was not. He was in the cockpit during the 1990s and knew the UN's limitations backwards. He was also committed to cost-cutting and internal reform.

For a while, Annan's tenure appeared golden. In 1998, he staved off an attack on Iraq by visiting Baghdad to negotiate with Saddam Hussein, returning to rapturous applause.[19] He took on the aura of an international celebrity – a new Dag Hammarskjöld – and in 2001 won the Nobel Peace Prize. Under Annan, the UN began to sharpen the position that the Charter could not be used to inhibit interventions to protect people in serious distress. While the UN had to sustain the principle of neutrality wherever possible, governments could not claim 'sovereignty' as a cover for violence against civilians. A doctrine of 'humanitarian intervention' began informally to be accepted; in 2005 it reached formal agreement as the 'responsibility to protect'.

But after 9/11, things began to deteriorate. The economic gap between North and South had fed a virulent strain of Muslim extremist rage, now vented on Western ideas and institutions. Its politics and terrorist methods could not be contained by any existing international security mechanisms. The new question was whether armed intervention against a state colluding with such extremists was justifiable to forestall palpable threats. This latest dynamic in international affairs is the most problematic since the rise of fascism in the 1930s, much more so than the state-based confrontation of the Cold War. How a set of inter-state mechanisms for international conflict resolution can be adapted for use in the 'war on terror' is a conundrum which may never be solved. Meanwhile the reactions of the US under George W Bush – whose administration made no secret of its disdain for multilateral diplomacy – plunged the UN into renewed crisis.

The 2002 war against the Taliban in Afghanistan found near-unanimous international support. But when the US wanted to launch a new war against Saddam Hussein – on the pretext that Iraq had failed to comply with UN resolutions demanding the elimination of all weapons of mass destruction – that was another matter. Since 1991, UN sanctions had been imposed on Iraq to promote the dismantling of its weapons program. The sanctions were controversial: the impact fell on civilians, not on Saddam's élite. So a program whereby Iraqi oil was traded for food and humanitarian aid was set up by the Security Council with oversight in the Secretariat. A UN weapons inspectorate managed to reduce significantly Iraqi capacity for building weapons, but left at the end of 1998 with sanctions still in place. In 2002, pumped-up US and UK intelligence on weapons capacity in Iraq was used as a pretext to call for a military invasion of Iraq on grounds of international security. By 2003, the hawks were raring to go in.

This was a seminal moment for the UN. Would the Security Council follow its earlier resolutions against Iraq with support for a US-led invasion? Despite arm-twisting, several Council members were reluctant and France threatened to use its veto. For millions around the world opposed to the war, the UN as a forum for settling international disputes would have lost all credibility if it had endorsed the military campaign. For many in the US, it lost all credibility by refusing. In 2004, Annan was pressed in a news conference to say whether the war was a legitimate act of 'peace enforcement' under the Charter. He replied that it was not – another UN news moment flashed around

Sources: Michael Howard, 'The Historical Development of the UN's Role in International Security', in Roberts & Kingsbury, op cit and www.iaea.org

Disarmament and nuclear non-proliferation

There is too little space to cover this component of 'international security' in detail. Article 11 of the UN Charter modestly empowered the General Assembly to include in its deliberations 'the principles governing disarmament and the regulation of armaments, and make recommendations'. The explosion of the first nuclear bomb plus Cold War antagonism propelled disarmament on to an altogether different plane, and led to resolutions demanding 'General and Complete Disarmament'. This denoted nuclear disarmament's starring role in the superpower grandstanding competition since neither had any intention of complying. A great deal of time and paper was wasted by a UN commission, General Assembly debates, two 'Disarmament Decades', and three Disarmament 'Special Sessions' in 1976, 1982 and 1988, none of which achieved much – except pave the way. When the US and USSR finally came to negotiate, they did so bilaterally.

Today, the organization associated with the control of nuclear weapons is the International Atomic Energy Authority (IAEA), based in Vienna. This autonomous intergovernmental body was set up by General Assembly resolution in 1957 and has a statutory UN linkage. It promotes the peaceful application of nuclear technology, attempts to inhibit its military use, provides safeguards against misuse, and encourages application of safety measures. The IAEA is held in high regard, and was awarded the Nobel Peace Prize in 2005. ∎

the globe. This not only cost Annan his US support, but efforts were subsequently made by US officials to throw mud at the UN and at him personally, to humiliate both and – at their most extreme – force Annan to resign.

Corruption was unearthed at the Iraqi Oil-for-Food program; but almost all of it was among the companies put forward by member states to gain lucrative contracts. Very little was in the Secretariat, and Annan himself was not connected; but his son had worked for a company that was. Eventually, Annan brought in a new Deputy, Mark Malloch-Brown, to help persuade Washington that damaging the UN at such a moment in world affairs was not in their interests. Annan – albeit damaged – stayed until his term expired in 2006. The latest Secretary-General, Ban

Ki Moon of Korea, is not likely to antagonize a US Administration any time soon. Whether the decisive influence of the US at the UN is regarded as its saving grace or as disgracefully compromising its actions, it is a fact of life. However uncomfortably, there must be accommodation with the US.

The energies of both Boutros-Ghali and Annan were heavily consumed by the need to adapt the precepts, principles and machinery of bodies developed in another age to the security – and development – needs of the contemporary world. Their impulse was the appalling suffering and dislocation of people in situations which the world and the UN could not ignore. Humanitarianism, subject of the next chapter, was in crisis.

1 James S Sutterlin, *The United Nations and the Maintenance of International Security: A Challenge to be Met* (second edition), Praeger, Westport Connecticut, 2003. **2** Stanley Meisler, *United Nations: The First Fifty Years*, Atlantic Monthly Press, New York, 1995. **3** Michael Howard, 'The UN and International Security', in Roberts and Kingsbury (Eds), *United Nations, Divided World*, Oxford, 1989. **4** United Nations website, accessed 5 November 2007. **5** Edward R Stettinius, *Report to the President on the San Francisco Conference*, US Department of State, 26 June 1945; quoted in Sutterlin, op cit. **6** Roberts and Kingsbury, op cit. p 5. **7** Daniel Patrick Moynihan, *A dangerous place*, Secker and Warburg, London, 1979. **8** Meisler, op cit. **9** Burton Yale Pines (ed), *A World without a UN*, The Heritage Foundation, Washington, 1982. **10** Jeffrey Harrod and Nico Schrijver, *The UN Under Attack*, Gower, Aldershot (UK), 1987. **11** Eric Hobsbawm, *Age of Extremes: The Short Twentieth Century, 1914-1991*, Michael Joseph, London, 1994. **12** Samuel P Huntington, *The Clash of Civilizations and the Remaking of World Order*, Simon and Schuster, 1996. **13** Javier Pérez de Cuéllar, *Anarchy or Order*, UN, New York, 1991, cited in Sutterlin op cit. **14** Boutros Boutros-Ghali, *An Agenda for Peace* (second edition), UN, New York, 1995. **15** Ibid, p 8. **16** Thomas G. Weiss et al (eds), *The United Nations and Changing World Politics* (fifth edition), Westview Press, 2007. **17** James S Sutterlin, op cit. **18** Ibid. **19** James Traub, *The Best Intentions: Kofi Annan and the UN in the Era of American Power*, Bloomsbury, London, 2006.

3 Rescue and relief

Humanitarian activity in the form of post-war relief was ingrained in the UN's mission. But its original operation fell foul of politics: UN aid could not be sent to countries in the communist bloc. Relief operations were subsequently conducted in wars and natural disasters by special UN bodies, some created for particular contexts, others for victim groups such as refugees. For many years, relief aid was seen as a soft issue, as welfare for the temporarily distressed and not central to the main UN tasks. As increasing numbers of people were affected by internal conflict in the 1980s and 1990s, relief became an important international security issue. Is there a 'humanitarian imperative' to intervene in certain situations? And should relief and rescue operations remain above the political divide?

IN TODAY'S WORLD, where innocent people suffering from the violence of war are unequivocally seen as a target of humanitarian relief, it is difficult to recapture the view that was standard during the 1939-45 war. This held that those on the enemy side were, to the last toddler and female octogenarian, complicit in hostilities. Except among Quakers and the International Red Cross, this idea was virtually universal. The doctrine of 'total war', championed by Winston Churchill and supported by the British Parliament, held that even if an allied country became over-run by Nazi Germany, relief should be prohibited because it would only help the enemy, whose responsibility it was to feed captive peoples.[1] Greece, to which this happened, was dependent for food on imports. Only a personal request by Franklin Roosevelt persuaded Churchill to allow ships under the Red Cross flag through the British naval blockade of German-occupied Greece, carrying food and medical supplies for starving civilians.[2] The accepted norms governing humanitarian relief have, thankfully, undergone a sea change since those days.

The UN operation predating the signing of the Charter was, as noted in chapter 1, the vast relief and rehabilitation effort for newly liberated countries in Europe. As the USSR consolidated its hold on Eastern Europe, this was wound up, and replaced by the 1947 US Marshall Plan for Western Europe only. But an important exception was conceded. Children in countries such as Poland were exempt, and relief to them under UN auspices could continue. The principle that there is no such thing as an enemy child was first articulated in 1919 by Eglantyne Jebb, founder of Save the Children UK.[3] Thus the notion of relief under neutral auspices for children was added to the principle already established by the International Red Cross, that those wounded or captured in battle should receive humanitarian aid.

At the UN, the superior claim of children to relief justified the creation of UNICEF in late 1946. From its inception, UNICEF asserted that children are above the political divide, providing relief in Eastern Europe and on both sides of post-1945 civil conflicts in China and Greece.[4] The UN had unwittingly provided itself with a Trojan Horse for circumventing the principle of sovereign integrity and non-intervention in internal disputes – a fact rarely noticed either by the public or by analysts of humanitarian affairs. Children are so 'non-political' that, in many minds, UNICEF has nothing to do with the UN at all.

Refugees and the displaced

The other immediate post-War humanitarian concern confronting the UN was the large numbers of European refugees left languishing in camps. The office of the UN High Commissioner for Refugees (UNHCR) took over this responsibility from the preexisting International Refugee Organization (IRO) by resolution of the General Assembly in 1950. Originally, neither the IRO or the UNHCR took on any role outside Europe. At the creation of Israel in 1948, a special body, the UN Relief and Works Agency (UNRWA), was set up to care for Palestinian refugees and continues to provide aid for displaced victims of conflict throughout the Middle East ($483 million in 2007[5]).

The 1951 Convention on Refugees is a landmark UN document of international law (see chapter 5). This establishes the right to protection and asylum of someone who flees their country because of a well-found fear of persecution due to race, religion, nationality, or membership of a particular social or political group.[6] This remains in force – although it is sometimes attacked as inappropriate for the contemporary era of large-scale migration and asylum application, and as vigorously defended by activists and organizations working on refugees' behalf. Certainly, it is often interpreted more narrowly than in the past, and inconsistently.[7]

UNHCR quickly became permanently established and expanded its mandate to assist refugees all over the world. By the 1980s it was handling large-scale relief operations for growing numbers of cross-border populations living in camps. During the 1990s, it assumed the leading UN role for internally displaced people (IDP). These are not strictly within its mission, but their situation is often as desperate. However, not all states will allow UNHCR to cross their borders to minister to the displaced. Since the 1980s, there has been a vast increase in both types of displaced populations, but today IDPs are much more numerous than refugees (as distinct from asylum seekers): 24.5 million compared to 9.9 million[8] (see map, page 58).

Like UNICEF, UNHCR developed over many years the particular kinds of expertise needed for humani-

Rescue and relief

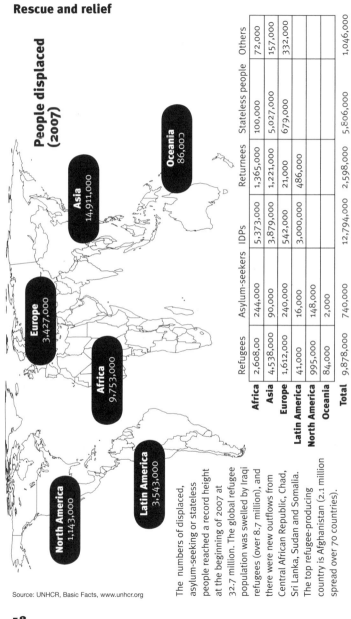

People displaced (2007)

The numbers of displaced, asylum-seeking or stateless people reached a record height at the beginning of 2007 at 32.7 million. The global refugee population was swelled by Iraqi refugees (over 8.7 million), and there were new outflows from Central African Republic, Chad, Sri Lanka, Sudan and Somalia. The top refugee-producing country is Afghanistan (2.1 million spread over 70 countries).

Source: UNHCR, Basic Facts, www.unhcr.org

	Refugees	Asylum-seekers	IDPs	Returnees	Stateless people	Others
Africa	2,608,00	244,000	5,373,000	1,365,000	100,000	72,000
Asia	4,538,000	90,000	3,879,000	1,221,000	5,027,000	157,000
Europe	1,612,000	240,000	542,000	21,000	679,000	332,000
Latin America	41,000	16,000	3,000,000	486,000		
North America	995,000	148,000				
Oceania	84,000	2,000				
Total	9,878,000	740,000	12,794,000	2,598,000	5,806,000	1,046,000

Map labels:

North America 1,143,000

Latin America 3,543,000

Africa 9,753,000

Europe 3,427,000

Asia 14,911,000

Oceania 86,000

tarian operations: procurement, shipping, transport, logistics, rations contents, and so on. But as its size grew, and its activities became more diffuse, its mandate for refugee protection became somewhat obscured. Within the UN system, it has taken the 'lead agency' role in delivering humanitarian relief to those displaced by war or persecution. Its rise to prominence is associated with post-Cold War conflicts, notably the Kurdish refugee crisis following the Gulf War (1991), and the crises in former Yugoslavia and Central Africa, of which more later.

Disaster relief

Disasters are described as 'natural' and 'man-made', although famines caused by political failure or war cannot easily be disentangled from those caused by the weather. People suffering from flood, earthquake or drought are palpably innocent of their plight; whereas in 'man-made' disasters, responsibilities are more clouded. In the 1960s, when NGOs and UN organizations took up a remodeled 'white man's burden' – humanitarian work in the developing world – such distinctions did not arise. The mission was projected by the publicity image of the starving child. Much confusion arose from the false portrayal of people in traditional subsistence economies as in a state of more or less permanent disaster. As television pictures began to dominate public perceptions, the compassionate impulse to help the disaster-ravaged fueled the mission and filled its collection boxes. But widespread hunger is rarely without a political cause, as economist Amartya Sen earned a Nobel Prize for explaining.[9]

One reaction to the scandal of half of humanity eating well while the other half appeared barely to eat at all was to redistribute food surpluses from richer countries. In 1961, George McGovern, Director of the US Food for Peace program, proposed the establishment of a multilateral food aid program under the

UN's Food and Agriculture Organization (FAO).[10] The World Food Programme (WFP) took over from bilateral arrangements an important role in food-stock accumulation and redistribution. A multilateral program meant that, should there be a clash, strategic considerations would not be used to define which populations were deemed to be in need and which were not. In fact, the concerns of major donors and their willingness (or not) to fund specific operations will always have an influence over the scale and desti-nation of relief goods. The WFP has since become the world's largest food aid operation, mostly supplying bulk food in emergencies, but also delivering rations for other humanitarian purposes, such as school meals in poor rural communities (see box opposite).

Many organizations whose reputations were built on their international 'mercy dash' image and the public generosity it generated – UNICEF, for example, and NGOs such as Oxfam – were troubled by the way in which this cast them as uniquely philanthropic. The role they wanted to play in the age of develop-ment was that of investors in the human condition, enabling people to develop their livelihoods and access basic health and other services, rather than simply tid-ing them over a crisis. Whether disaster relief was the antithesis of development or on the same continuum has generated much debate, especially since theories of dependency emerged from Latin America in the 1960s and 1970s. This topic is resumed in the next chapter, but it is important to note here that words such as 'humanitarian' and 'relief' have often carried pejorative, neocolonial and do-gooding connotations. This had an important influence on the more muscu-lar ideas associating 'humanitarian principles' with 'human rights' that proliferated in the 1990s along with the surge in 'man-made' emergencies.

For relief in 'natural' disaster situations, the UN originally set up a Disasters Relief Office in the

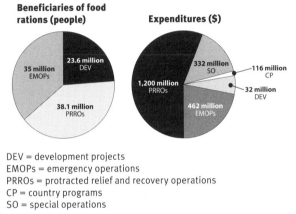

WFP: the peak year of 2005

2005 was seen by the World Food Programme as the most challenging year since the Second World War in humanitarian aid terms. Some 2.2 million victims of the Indian Ocean tsunami required food aid; in Africa there were food crises in Niger (locust plague) and Darfur; in August/September Hurricanes Katrina and Stan (the latter affecting 1.5 million in Guatemala); and in October the major earthquake in Kashmir, Pakistan.

Beneficiaries of food rations (people)

35 million EMOPs

23.6 million DEV

38.1 million PRROs

Expenditures ($)

332 million SO

116 million CP

1,200 million PRROs

32 million DEV

462 million EMOPs

DEV = development projects
EMOPs = emergency operations
PRROs = protracted relief and recovery operations
CP = country programs
SO = special operations

Source: World Food Programme annual report 2005 www.wfp.org

Secretariat. It had few resources, and its contribution on the scene of earthquakes and similar crises was negligible. In some circumstances, for example to address the devastation in the new state of Bangladesh in 1971, a special UN operation was mounted (as for the creation of Israel in 1948); when the crisis ended, so did the operation. The UN Secretariat also solicits funds from member states for emergency operations designated to a 'lead agency'. But actual relief work is undertaken by the bodies with appropriate mandates.

Baptisms of fire

The crisis which confronted the evolving international system with the awkward truth about the political nature of relief, and the impossibility of sustaining the non-intervention principle in conflict situations, was the 1967-70 Nigerian civil war. This is seen as the start of modern emergency aid.

The eastern part of the country – the part with all the oil – tried to secede from Nigeria as independent Biafra. The Nigerian Federal army blockaded Biafra to end the secession. The Organization of African Unity (OAU), committed to the integrity of state borders, backed the Federalists. But eastern Nigeria was full of Christian missionaries, who begged humanitarian allies in the West to bring aid to starving Biafrans by breaking the blockade. Federal Nigeria regarded this as political support for the rebels. The UN, bound to the non-intervention principle, was unable to act. Secretary-General U Thant turned to UNICEF. With the International Committee of the Red Cross (ICRC), UNICEF negotiated the precarious acceptance of relief airlifts – most food was from the US and the planes were flown by an assortment of humanitarian daredevils – through the blockade. Eventually, the rebellion was crushed and Biafra re-absorbed into Nigeria with no bloodbath repercussions. There has always been debate over whether the airlifts prolonged the war and ultimately made things worse. Humanitarians are much given to *mea culpa*, but in the depths of famine this is an impossible call to make. That they were naïve, and exploited by Biafran leaders for propaganda purposes, is undeniable.[11]

The Nigerian experience illustrated the importance of neutrality in humanitarian affairs. Only because UNICEF and the ICRC were seen as impartial providers of aid based only on criteria of need were planes not shot out of the sky. Ten years later, UNICEF and the ICRC once again partnered the leadership of a large international humanitarian operation to which many UN bodies contributed, this time in Cambodia (Kampuchea), which was supposedly famine-torn.

Here, the politics were even more fraught. Vietnam – still a Western pariah state – had invaded Cambodia in 1979 to eject the murderous Pol Pot, and the UN did not recognize the replacement regime. Once again, the NGOs took the side of 'illegal' authorities, and agreed not to assist those fleeing their control. Once again, they failed to appreciate that only by upholding the principle of neutrality can humanitarians gain access to civilians hostage to 'the other side'. It turned out that those crossing the border into Thailand and seeking relief in camps run by another special UN operation were in a much worse state than those in the Cambodian countryside.[12]

These two historical examples concern war-induced emergencies. But there can be famine crises not associated with conflict in which politics deeply intrude. Many states refuse to admit to famine, or even to cholera epidemic, because of national pride. The Ethiopian famine of 1974 was exposed by a British television documentary informed by NGOs; UN organizations had accepted Emperor Haile Selassie's assurance that reports of starvation were exaggerated. His disdain for human life sparked a revolution that cost him his throne. Ten years later, in another Ethiopian famine, NGOs again shamed the international community into commensurate humanitarian action – as they had also done, never mind their lack of neutrality, in Nigeria and Cambodia. Their response arose from compassion, and from overwhelming public pressure on 'the world', especially its only common set of institutions, the UN, which seemed achingly slow to act on behalf of people visibly dying on the nightly television news.

The NGOs thus forced open the debate leading to the acceptance of new humanitarian norms. On behalf of suffering humanity, 'We the peoples' insisted that diplomats and international civil servants cease clinging to the wreckage of the sovereignty principle, and put some urgency, punch and effectiveness into the UN's rescue and relief capacity.

Taking centre stage

In 1985, at the height of the second Ethiopian famine, the UN accepted that it was no longer adequate to co-opt UNICEF as 'lead agency' when humanitarian operations were confronted with serious political difficulty. A special Office for Emergency Operations for Africa (OEOA) was set up in the Secretariat, marking the start of the UN's assumption of overall responsibility for humanitarian relief. In 1991, the General Assembly authorized the new position of Under-Secretary-General for emergency activity. In 1992, a Department of Humanitarian Affairs (DHA) was set up; in 1998 this became the Office for the Co-ordination of Humanitarian Affairs (OCHA). These new developments marked an entirely different level of UN attention to humanitarian crisis. Instead of being cast as marginal welfarists, humanitarians had moved centre stage in international affairs. But their embrace by the political fold was a decidedly mixed blessing.

As in any situation where one body is set up to co-ordinate the work of much larger and more experienced bodies (in this case UNHCR, UNICEF and WFP), especially when speed and effectiveness on the ground is essential, there were difficulties and much treading on toes. There was also confusion among some UN diplomats and bureaucrats, who imagined that operations on the ground, as well as on the political and fundraising front, could be managed by DHA. Sadako Ogata, the UN High Commissioner for Refugees (1991-2001), had to argue tenaciously that it was essential that UNHCR retain 'lead agency' role in Bosnia, for example.[13] Organizational strengths and mandates need to be deployed in a co-ordinated framework, not superseded by a humanitarian tsar or tied down by red tape. In addition, the importance of NGO emergency relief activity, and the pressures exerted by media exposure, weighed heavily against the tendency at the UN Secretariat to examine crisis response through the lens of relations between states and agonize over Charter principles.[14]

Relief operations tend to be somewhat chaotic. Many organizations are scrambling to the rescue of victims, some with more zeal than acumen or experience. Where order has broken down – which happens in situations that are peaceful but devastated, as well as where there is violence or warfare – losses and inefficiencies are unavoidable. The idea of a streamlined 'system' co-ordinated by a UN supremo whose emergency 'legions' are the various UN organizations with their specializations, supplemented by NGO foot soldiers, is impracticable. The emergency situation is volatile and relief personnel of different disciplines, backgrounds and organizational affiliations cannot function as if they were an army under central control. What a top UN official can do is to negotiate the modalities for a relief operation with the parties in political or military control. For those on the ground, co-ordination involves liaison as well as avoiding inconsistencies and duplication. As everyone piled into the debate on the improvement of the UN's humanitarian response, institutional and technical difficulties became conflated with political issues, exacerbating the problem of dealing with either.[15]

The humanitarian high tide

The fusion of humanitarian and political crisis reached its zenith in the early 1990s. There was a historical high of 29 in the number of wars in 1992-93. Although most were in developing countries, war had also returned to Europe for the first time since the 1940s.[16] UN Secretary-General Boutros-Ghali had laid out his vision of UN conflict-related activity in *An Agenda for Peace* in June 1992, covering preventive diplomacy, peacekeeping and building, and post-conflict rehabilitation. The premise for all of these types of activity was cast as 'humanitarian'. This word, normally used for a 'soft' task, had now been co-opted as the means of undermining the obstacle of the sovereignty principle to justify intervention in a state's (or failed state's) affairs – a political purpose. Since there were over-expectations about the role of the UN in the post-Cold War world, pitfalls associated with this proposition were overlooked.

An important precedent had been set following the Gulf War. This had led to the flight of 1.5 million Kurdish refugees into the mountains on Iraq's border with Turkey. In April 1991, the Security Council passed a landmark resolution (No 688) linking the violation of human rights to threats to international peace and security.[17] This demanded that immediate access be allowed to those in need of assistance 'in all parts of Iraq'. Instead of the standard UN procedure of seeking consent from national authorities to enter their territory to reach those in distress, Iraq's sovereignty would be ignored. The coalition forces then intervened militarily to create a safety zone in northern Iraq, and the UNHCR became 'lead agency' for a relief operation for the Kurds. This operation helped establish a virtually separate political administration in Kurdish northern Iraq. This was a success, but too much was read into the contribution of humanitarian effort to the political settlement. Coalition forces made it practicable, and Iraq remained vulnerable to attack if it attempted aggression in the Kurdish zone. These factors put this humanitarian operation into a special league: it was internationally enforced, politically and militarily.

As crises proliferated, the huge burden placed on international relief activity, as well as its potential derailment by one or another kind of political intrusion, became more evident. Take the UN operations in the Balkans. In early 1992, Bosnia-Herzegovina seceded from Yugoslavia under Slobodan Milosevic. Within months the Bosnian Serbs – with Milosevic's backing – took up arms against Muslim and Croat compatriots to carve out their own territorial entity linked to Serbia, and set in motion their infamous pol icy of 'ethnic cleansing'. Bosnian Muslims did not flee to escape attack; they were driven out of their homes as a purpose of war, and confined in camps where they suffered extreme privation, rape and brutality.

Although the UN sent peacekeeping forces (UNPROFOR), they had no Security Council mandate to contain Serbian aggression by military means. Instead, they were charged with keeping open Sarajevo airport to allow in relief, and with protecting relief convoys trying to reach populations under siege. This placed the humanitarian operation in a position where it tacitly accepted the Serbian military onslaught and the war crimes to which the Muslim population were exposed. In this situation, it was impossible to talk of 'humanitarian neutrality'. As the conflict continued without resolution, the UN's political effort not to take sides meant, effectively, doing just that.

The UN's humanitarian machinery was stretched to its limits on the ground. No-one could doubt the courage of UNHCR personnel who tirelessly negotiated food convoys through road blocks and unstable 'peace corridors'. Relief workers were beginning to lose their lives – even becoming targets – in this and other conflicts, partly because political and humanitarian efforts had become entangled. A more disastrous result was that UNHCR's relief program was co-opted into becoming a tool for making Bosnian civilians stay in their homes or in 'UN safe areas' – a policy way beyond any interpretation of its mandate for refugees. The hope was that the sum total of the international humanitarian presence would be enough to deter 'ethnic cleansing'. The UN DHA thought that political, military, and humanitarian objectives could be 'carried out effectively in integrated and unified operations.'[18] They were wrong.

The UN contingents became hostage to the Serbs, with the military personnel unable to take decisive action for fear of retaliation against the relief program.[19] This was quite unlike Iraq in 1991, or Somalia in 1992, where considerable armed force was used to bring in relief. In Bosnia, as earlier in Nigeria, the humanitarian operation – seen as buying time for negotiating a ceasefire and a political settlement which remained out of reach – became blamed for continuing the suffering, and cast as partisan. Without the backing of armed intervention against the aggressor, this strategy eventually collapsed. The Bosnian-Serb massacre of 8,000 people at Srebrenica in 1995, with UN peacekeepers standing helplessly by, spelled doom to the idea that humanitarian activity can be any kind of substitute for standing down warlords by force. UN efforts to bring about a political settlement failed; only when NATO bombardment and a US initiative led to the 1995 Dayton Accords did the prospect of peace in Bosnia emerge.

African horrors

In a book of this length, it is impossible to review all the recent and current conflict emergencies in sub-Saharan Africa and assess the UN response. The litany is grisly: Angola, Rwanda, Burundi, Somalia, Southern Sudan, Congo, Sierra Leone, Liberia, Darfur (northern and western Sudan), as well as other scenes of turmoil or persecution in which there have been displacements and death, as in Togo, Senegal, Zimbabwe and Kenya. Political and financial considerations, reflected in actions of the Security Council and other essentially diplomatic bodies, continue to limit the scope of humanitarian relief operations. And these often suffer from technical shortcomings and financial waste. But blaming humanitarian operations for the failure of warring parties to reach or honor a ceasefire, or for failure by the international diplomatic community to impose security militarily, is absurd. Wars continue until the parties cease waging them, not because relief workers are trying to keep civilians alive.

The world's crisis response capacity continues to grow and a large literature has built up in retrospective evaluations of specific operations. Some commentators seem more intent on finding neocolonial conspiracies and moral turpitude behind the deficiencies of international relief than in perceiving the extreme difficulties on the ground. Some condemnations of humanitarian operations – by Alex de Waal, for example – have harked back to Churchill's dictum that it is preferable not to help starving people because this inhibits them from throwing off unjust regimes.[20] The spectacle of regime-less chaos – as in Somalia, Congo, Sierra Leone, where warlords willfully destroyed all government and civil structures and perpetrated human rights violations on an appalling scale – discounts this thesis. Many such critics forget that, as recently as the Second World War, similar brutality was routinely meted out to civilian populations in Europe, and – other than Quakers and the International Red Cross – no-one thought of going to their aid. On the basis of human suffering, that war should have been brought to an end long before Germany or Japan surrendered. The UN's existence has helped to change the international moral dynamic. But it has also enhanced expectations: when humanity is in desperate straits, the UN must *do something*.

Certain cases illustrate the increasingly complex predicaments humanitarians face. After the 1994 Rwandan genocide, two million Hutus fled into what was then eastern Zaire, with vanquishing Tutsi forces hard on their heels. This produced one of the most violent and confused refugee situations imaginable. Extremists responsible for the genocide were among those seeking humanitarian aid. The many relief organizations helping in the camps were faced with the dilemma that part of their aid was going to war criminals re-arming against the new Rwandan regime. Médecins sans Frontières (MSF) and the International Red Cross pulled out on the basis that their aid was compromised. UNHCR and others remained, as they did not want to withdraw assistance from genuine refugees being held hostage by armed militias.

This dilemma confronts relief operators wherever no adequate security force is provided by the host country or internationally to protect camp residents and police the program. International provision of such a force depends on the willingness of the host government to accept it, as well as the willingness of donors to provide it.[21] Neither may be forthcoming. This situation – an inadequate UN and Pan-African force, Sudanese non-cooperation, and an over-stretched relief operation in constant jeopardy – is the case in Darfur at present. A peace enforcement action under Chapter VII as for Somalia in 1992 would require Security Council approval, which China opposes.

Humanitarians plow on

Conflicts, wars and human rights have conferred on humanitarian relief its recent enhanced attention. The UN's willingness to navigate the barrier of sovereignty seemed, initially, to favor its increased commitment to humanitarian assistance. But the integration of diplomatic action, peacekeeping, human rights monitoring, and relief turned out to be a mistake. Once parties to a conflict see humanitarian aid as politically tainted or treat it as a weapon of war, the possibility of defending the inalienable right of ordinary people to survival may be lost. Human rights are supposed to be indivisible and their violation has increasingly been used to support arguments for military intervention. But in the midst of starvation and death, the right to survive should predominate for all practicable purposes, and a useful response to that is indistinguishable from a response to desperate human need on the more straightforward basis of old-fashioned mercy.

The principle of humanitarian neutrality – aid purely on the basis of human need – has been jeopardized by the politicization of humanitarian affairs. The attempt to justify and shape humanitarian action to fit the fashionable framework of human rights – itself a loaded agenda as far as many non-Western countries are concerned, and one the ICRC and French humanitarian organizations strenuously avoid – has arguably made things worse. The only practical point of citing human rights violations is to indicate breaches of international law. What does that achieve for victims? MSF believes that supporting the right of military intervention on humanitarian grounds is simply a way of masking a deliberate political choice with gestures of generosity and compassion.[22] In addition, if the word 'humanitarian' is used to justify armed aggression, genuine humanitarians may be unable to function. No-one will take seriously the humanitarian credentials of an organization whose other arm is bombing them. Neither the Red Cross flag nor a blue 'UN' logo provides the guarantee of safety, either for personnel or for relief supplies, that they once did.

Repeated efforts to improve the performance of UN emergencies machinery led in 2006 to trials with a 'cluster approach', whereby different UN agencies take responsibility for certain areas: WHO, with a new 'Health Action in Crises' program, takes the lead in health, UNICEF in nutrition plus water and sanitation, WFP in logistics and so on. It is too early to say whether this allows more people to receive more cost-effective and appropriate relief, but the UN center, committed to 'humanitarian reform', believes so.[23]

In reality, UNICEF – focused on those non-political beings, children – remains the most engaged and the most effective as far as delivery of basic education, water, sanitation, health and other services is concerned (see box). Specialized agencies and others play a role within the UN-coordinated or 'cluster' framework. But with the exception of UNHCR and WFP, most do little (though WHO does more than it did). In some situations, for example in Somalia, and in southern Senegal where armed rebels have been trying to secede for 18 years, UNICEF has the only significant international presence.[24] UNICEF is far from politically innocent; over decades it has learned how to be politically astute in championing children's needs. It is also expert in program delivery, and has suitable staff and resources. The UN itself is remote from any emergency scene. UNHCR has scaled down its humanitarian operations since the days of Sadako Ogata and now focuses on repatriation of the displaced. Most UN organizations are johnnies-

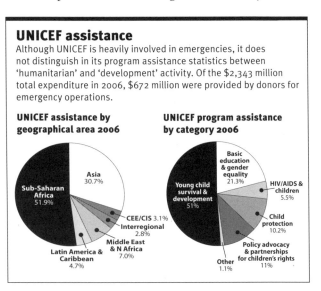

UNICEF assistance

Although UNICEF is heavily involved in emergencies, it does not distinguish in its program assistance statistics between 'humanitarian' and 'development' activity. Of the $2,343 million total expenditure in 2006, $672 million were provided by donors for emergency operations.

UNICEF assistance by geographical area 2006

- Sub-Saharan Africa 51.9%
- Asia 30.7%
- CEE/CIS 3.1%
- Interregional 2.8%
- Middle East & N Africa 7.0%
- Latin America & Caribbean 4.7%

UNICEF program assistance by category 2006

- Young child survival & development 51%
- Basic education & gender equality 21.3%
- HIV/AIDS & children 5.5%
- Child protection 10.2%
- Policy advocacy & partnerships for children's rights 11%
- Other 1.1%

come-lately to the humanitarian business. They were not set up to work that way, as we shall see.

Natural disasters, which do not attract so much analytic attention since they are so much less sexy than wars, should not be forgotten. Cyclones, floods, and other meteorologically based disasters are becoming more common in the face of climate change. Preparedness and early warning systems, as well as logistics, management and communications, will require increased attention. After the 2004 tsunami, the UN's Office for the Coordination of Humanitarian Affairs was credited with raising funds and unblocking obstacles to the largest relief operation ever[25]. Disaster relief and rehabilitation after such emergencies have much in common with international development assistance, the subject we shall turn to next.

1 Winston Churchill, Speech, 20 August 1940; Hansard, Parliamentary Debates, Vol 364, 1161. **2** Maggie Black, *A cause for our times*, Oxfam and OUP, 1992. **3** www.savethechildren.net/alliance/about_us/history.html **4** Maggie Black, *The Children and the Nations*, UNICEF and Macmillan Australia, 1987. **5** www.un.org/unrwa/finances/index.html **6** www.unhcr.org/basics.html **7** Jamie Doward and Mark Townsend, 'Just one in six of Iraq's refugees is accepted', *The Observer*, 7 October 2007. **8** www.unhcr.org **9** Amartya Sen, *Poverty and Famines*, OUP 1987; and (with Jean Dreize) *The Political Economy of Hunger*, OUP 1991. **10** www.wfp.org **11** Black, *A cause for our times* and *The Children and the Nations*, op cit. **12** Black, op cit; also William Shawcross, *The Quality of Mercy*, Simon and Schuster, New York, 1984. **13** Sadako Ogata, *The Turbulent Decade*, WW Norton, 2005. **14** Michael Barnett, *Eyewitness to a Genocide*, Cornell University Press, 2002. **15** Angela Penrose, 'UN Humanitarian Machinery', in Erskine Childers (ed), *Challenges to the United Nations*, CIIR and St. Martin's Press, UK, 1994. **16** Larry Minear and Thomas G Weiss, *Mercy under Fire*, Westview, 1995. **17** Sadako Ogata, 'A Challenge to the United Nations: A Humanitarian Perspective', Lecture to the Centre for Global Governance, LSE, University of London, May 1993. **18** Angela Penrose, op cit. **19** Stanley Meisler, *United Nations: The First Fifty Years*, Atlantic Monthly Press, 1995. **20** Thomas G Weiss and Cindy Collins, *Humanitarian challenges and intervention*, Westview, 2000. **21** Thomas G Weiss et al, *The United Nations and Changing World Politics* (fifth ed), Westview, 2007. **22** David Rieff, 'Humanitarianism in Crisis', in *Foreign Affairs*, Vol 81, No 6, Nov-Dec 2002. **23** *UNICEF Humanitarian Report 2007*, UNICEF New York, February 2007. **24** Personal visit to Ziguinchor, Casamance, southern Senegal, March 2007. **25** Thomas G Weiss, 2007 op cit.

4 UN development assistance: good, bad or indifferent?

The idea of 'development' is essentially a post-colonial construct. When decolonization took off, the institutions of the UN began to be applied in earnest to the second key purpose for which they were created: the promotion of better living standards worldwide. The UN Secretariat had its own Department of Economic Affairs; there were specialized agencies for sectoral activities; and a new body was set up in 1965, the UN Development Programme (UNDP). Other funds and programs were spawned whenever new development-related issues – population, environment, women's equality, HIV/AIDS – rose to prominence. But after a crescendo in the 1970s, the UN's voice on economic development fell silent. In the 1990s, the UN rediscovered lack of development as a threat to world peace, and in 2000 member states agreed a set of Millennium Development Goals at a special UN Summit. So what is the UN's record in advancing 'better living standards' in the world's poorer corners?

AFTER THE COLD War crippled much UN activity in the political arena, its organizations began to seek a new international role by applying themselves to the process of decolonization. Using its non-imperialist credentials to midwife the political and economic institutions of 'emerging' nations, and assuming the task of 'international development' via multinational assistance, provided the UN with a new *raison d'être*. The first 'UN Development Decade' was declared by President John F Kennedy at the UN in New York immediately following his 1961 Washington inauguration. He spoke inspirationally: 'To those peoples in the huts and villages of half the globe struggling to break the bonds of mass misery, we pledge our best efforts to help them help themselves… If a free society cannot help the poor, it can never serve the few who are rich.'

The political impulse behind the enthusiasm for 'development' in the newly independent countries in Asia, the Caribbean, the Pacific, and Africa was the fear that they would fall under Soviet influence unless their bread was buttered by the West. But, nonetheless, the mission was charged with idealism. The spectacle of people living without any of the appurtenances of modern industrialized life and apparently on the brink of starvation caught the imagination of people in the West. The new mission was taken up with alacrity: the relief of hunger and deprivation was *the* cause for the times. Thus was born the notion of 'aid', a type of public expenditure previously only used for fostering strategic or military allies, but now imbued with humanitarian promise. UN member states agreed a target, that every industrialized country should devote one per cent (later reduced to 0.7 per cent) of their GNP to Official Development Assistance (ODA). These transfers would bolster embryonic economies and enable the welfare state to be writ large upon an international canvas, making the world a more just, humane, and equal place.[1] Fanciful? Perhaps no more so than the quest for peace.

A problem besetting the new mission, then as now, concerned what actually constituted this 'development' that the new countries and their richer partners were trying to bring about. When the UN issued its first report on 'Economic Development of Under-developed Countries' in 1950, no attempt was made to explain what was meant by the term: it was thought to be self-evident.[2] The model for achieving development via 'aid' was the Marshall Plan; but for the developing world this was irrelevant. In Europe, there had been huge devastation of infrastructure, but once rebuilding and economic regeneration began, there was an educated population and know-how of all kinds. This was not the case in large parts of Asia and Latin America, and least of all in Africa where a modern infrastructure and cadres to run it had to be constituted almost from scratch. Development could not simply be slapped down on pre-industrial societies courtesy of aid. Although the per capita GNP of developing countries grew on average by five per cent during the 1960s (largely due to continuing high prices for raw materials), the Development Decade was a letdown. Many projects failed and almost no new wealth trickled down to poorer citizens.

In 1969, Lester Pearson, ex-Prime Minister of Canada and chair of a 'Grand Assize' into the Decade's results, reported that 'the climate surrounding foreign aid programs is heavy with disillusion and distrust'.[3] Pearson pointed out that development could not be uniform for countries of disparate size, potential and existing organization. He also pointed out that, over and above economic advance, development had certain common features: social progress, redistribution of wealth, efficient administration, political stability and democratic participation. Here was the crux of the matter. Was 'development' simply to do with industrialization and economic growth? Or did it have a broader character, in which social and political values played a part? This debate was to run and run before, decades later, the UN made up its collective mind and committed its institutions to the attack on poverty in all its manifestations.

UN 'development' mechanisms

When the UN Charter was elaborated, much more effort was put into designing the Security Council than the Economic and Social Council (ECOSOC) – the core body primarily responsible for promoting 'higher standards of living, full employment, and conditions of social and economic progress and development' (Article 55). The great powers made sure of their control of the Security Council, but decisions in ECOSOC were by majority vote. If the Big Five, especially the US, had thought that matters affecting their vital interests were at stake, they would surely have given themselves a veto.[4] Any idea that the IMF and the World Bank Group would report to ECOSOC or be 'co-ordinated' by it was illusory. According to the Charter, these bodies were to be 'brought into a relationship' with the UN, and they succeeded in making this relationship extremely distant from the start. Their structures were different, power was held within them by the leading capitalist nations, and nothing they did was ever put to majority vote in ECOSOC. When they came to consider 'development', their views were dominated by ideas of economic growth and financial stability. With some deviations – by World Bank Presidents Robert McNamara (1968-81) and James Wolfensohn (1995-2005) – the state of developing country economies, not peoples, has been their lodestar ever since.

ECOSOC, through the Secretariat's Department of Economic Affairs ('Social' was later added, making it DESA), was also supposed to 'co-ordinate' the work of various international organizations which might have some bearing on development – the World Meteorological Organization, for example – but whose relationship with the UN was as remote as the World Bank's. ECOSOC was also supposed to co-ordinate the work of the specialized agencies, including the Food and Agriculture Organization (FAO), the International Labour Organization (ILO), the UN Educational, Scientific and Cultural Organization (UNESCO), and the World Health Organization (WHO). These clearly had a role to play in the social and economic advancement of peoples in developing countries. But they all operated autonomously. WHO did not even have a unified structure within itself: powerful regional health bodies such as the Pan-African Health Organization (PAHO) set their own policy and agenda. We will come on to the specialized agencies in a moment. But what, then, was left for ECOSOC (the diplomats) or DESA (their servants, the bureaucrats) to contribute to 'international development'?

ECOSOC did not oversee development-related funds and programs such as UNICEF, UNDP, the UN Environment Programme (UNEP) or the UN Population Fund (UNFPA), which reported to the General Assembly. However, it did and does 'co-ordinate' a number of regional commissions – the Economic Commission for Asia and the Pacific (ESCAP), for example, and others for Africa, Latin America and so on. These pull together economic and social data and grind out reports, assessments and forecasts in their own locations. Special Commissions concerned with topics of developmental importance have also been created down the years, such as the Commission on Sustainable Development (UNCSD), set up after the first Earth Summit at Rio de Janeiro in 1992. These are known as 'functional' ECOSOC Commissions, but some are moribund and few have played any 'functional' role in international development. In most cases, their job is to follow up the outcome documents of international conferences on their topics, convene meetings, and commission reports.

In short, ECOSOC has been something of a dumping ground for institutionally homeless causes. The Security Council's decision-making role *vis à vis* political security has never been assigned to ECOSOC in relation to 'economic security', 'development co-operation', or even human rights, whose machinery it also oversaw until very recently. In 1993, Maurice Bertrand, for many years chief of the UN's Joint Inspection Unit and a distinguished voice from inside the system on its shortcomings, described ECOSOC as in a state of permanent crisis for many decades, lacking credibility or authority.[5]

Its own development program

The key UN instrument for practical development co-operation – meaning programs and projects on the ground – was supposed to be the UN Development Programme (UNDP), which came into being in 1965. UNDP was an amalgamation of two existing UN bodies – a Fund (SUNFED) for providing loans, and another providing technical assistance. They had failed to do anything much, mainly because industrialized countries would not stump up significant resources, preferring to provide this kind of support via the World Bank or specialized agencies. The heads of the two earlier organizations – Paul Hoffman and David Owen – provided dynamic leadership of UNDP in its early days.

However, for internal structural reasons, and because it never managed to adapt its mission to the challenges facing 'development' as they evolved, either analytically or practically, UNDP's overall performance can be generously described as disappointing. In many countries, UNDP programs have mostly been unconnected to any real poverty eradication agenda and contact with the lives of people in the predicament it was supposed to address has been negligible. Infrastructure in which UNDP invested and technical projects its funds supported might help the country but not necessarily the poor. This did not stop UNDP making a bid to become co-ordinator of all UN development co-operation on the ground during the UN reforms of the 1990s. Because 'co-ordination' and 'lack of duplication' are beloved by UN donors, this bid partially succeeded: there is now one overall country program under the UNDP Resident Co-ordinator, in which all UN organizations make their separate contributions while trying to unify their approach. Coherence of development plans and policies within a country are also better assured through a World Bank-led 'poverty reduction strategy' process. But to many poverty activists, this remains suspect since it is geared to the Bank's market-based prescriptions about what development consists of and how poverty is to be conquered.

In the 1990s, UNDP midwifed the articulation of a poverty-centered vision of development in its annual *Human Development Reports*. Its own programs and internal structure have recently been reformed, but the jury is still out on whether they provide an effective means of delivering on this vision. Today UNDP claims to be building national and local capacity for governance, especially in post-conflict societies. However, its organizational culture remains metropolitan and insufficiently grounded in genuine field-based perspectives.

The specialized agencies

The UN's specialized agencies for food, agriculture, education, health and labor were in no way set up to run the kind of projects associated with an NGO or UNICEF development mission, which is essentially motivated by humanitarian values. The agencies predate the founding of the UN, let alone decolonization, and were not designed to address directly the deprived situation of people living in pre-industrial or semi-subsistence economies. It is important to recognize this because otherwise wrong assumptions and judgments are made about what they do and whether they perform well. They exist to provide 'technical assistance': advice and scientific know-how, and to circulate information. Thus an agency such as FAO is expected to harness the best and latest information on food and agriculture (irrigation, fisheries, forestry, livestock, crop science, nutrition and so on) – already a vast undertaking – and put it at the disposal of 'the nations'. At the time the agencies were created, the international sharing and distribution of knowledge in this way was a brave and radical adventure.

The specialized agencies are therefore rather like multicultural technical institutes. Most of their expertise is in their headquarters. Staff in 'the field' are usually there because the country in question does not yet have that kind of expertise; or the expert has been lent to a government body to help devise a new policy or program. This may help boost national productivity, introduce new technology, or influence who gets trained to do what; but the impact on the condition of people in poverty is incidental. It is assumed to be beneficial – as if all development is positive and politically neutral, which can never be the case – and the task is to make sure the job is technically well done, not consider the political or social implications. Those outcomes will depend on the policies of the country in question, and most countries regard their choice of development path as part of their sovereign right not to have their internal affairs questioned by neo-colonialist outsiders.

The agencies respect that idea. They rarely help implement services, and efforts are targeted to poor areas only when the recipient government agrees. They do not have a coherent anti-poverty strategy, even if the predicament of 'underdevelopment' is their *raison d'être*. They may say that they do – certainly they cite the statistics of hunger, disease and miserable livelihoods to justify their activities; but what they actually do on the ground rarely bears out this promise.

Some of the agencies at certain times have tried to direct their energies and use their influence to address poverty, or help especially deprived populations, directly. In the 1960s, FAO – with ECOSOC's endorsement – ran an international drive for 'Freedom from Hunger' in partnership with other UN bodies and NGOs worldwide, which succeeded in implanting the idea of aid for the 'hungry millions' in the public mind of the Western world and gave an important boost to the development mission. From 1967, WHO tooled up its international vaccination program to undertake a campaign to eradicate smallpox; the last identified victim was in 1977, and in 1979 the world was declared smallpox-free. The UN often cites this as one of its successes, mainly profiting those populations who suffer worst from the debilitating diseases affecting the world's less fortunate citizens. A subsequent campaign to eradicate polio has not yet fully succeeded. Others against tuberculosis and malaria are ongoing.

During the 1970s and early 1980s, WHO Director-General Halfdan Mahler spearheaded a movement for 'health by the people', which encouraged Ministries of Health all over the developing world to re-orient their limited healthcare resources and personnel away from expensive high-tech hospitals and towards basic services for poorer citizens. This initiative derived much of its radical thinking from 'alternative' ideas circulating at that time (see below).This priority slipped heavily when Mahler was unexpectedly voted out in 1988 by the African majority in the World Health Assembly and replaced by Hiroshi Nakajima of Japan, one of the most autocratic of agency chiefs. Nakajima was forced out in 1997 under heavy criticism from donors and replaced by Gro Harlem Brundtland of Norway. WHO has since recovered much of its reputation.

UNESCO also endured a dreadful period, under the leadership of Amadou M'Bow, recounted in chapter 2. Edouard Saouma of Lebanon, Director-General of FAO from 1976-1993 was in the same league. So poorly was FAO regarded that, in 1977, a separate International Fund for Agricultural Development (IFAD) was set up to address rural poverty: its record is better. In 1991, *The Ecologist* published an issue entitled *The FAO: Promoting World Hunger*, with excoriating articles by eminent figures such as environmentalist Vandana Shiva, and a pseudonymous article by a senior FAO official. He wrote: 'FAO, set up to *develop* world agriculture so as to enable the world to feed itself, has disastrously failed in its task. It has ignored and even derided traditional agricultural methods and permits no international criticism of its policy of promoting Western-style intensive farming and the export of cash crops. FAO's performance is judged on the amount of money it spends, not on the effectiveness of its projects, it ignores the voices of the people it is supposed to be helping and it has close links with agribusiness internationals, whose products it actively promotes.'[6] WHO faced similar criticism under Nakajima for its close links to the multinational pharmaceutical industry. In 2005, FAO commissioned its first ever independent external evaluation. Published in 2007, the report described the organization as in 'a financial and program crisis', suffering from a heavy and costly bureaucracy, inflexibility and risk-aversion, declining capacity and loss of 'core competencies'.[7] FAO's staff immediately petitioned the management to implement the evaluators' recommendations.

Despite justifiable criticisms of the specialized agencies – the ILO is arguably the most bureaucratic of all, and as unconnected to the lives of its constituency – some run many valuable programs and projects. Dedicated and hard-working professionals manage against strong practical and institutional odds to achieve good results – on HIV/AIDS research, disease control, the elimination of child labor, 'education for all' – and circulate information to parts of the world that desperately need it. But it is rare to find a coherent view of development as it relates to their sector or how to contribute to it effectively, other than by issuing reports and spending money in the developing world; or, in ILO's case, by elaborating Conventions on work and workers that cannot realistically be implemented in an impoverished country setting. 'Technical assistance' on its own is of questionable value in seriously poor environments. Active participation in programs and projects by beneficiaries – seen by NGOs as critical to developmental success – is more often the exception than the rule.

UN development assistance: good, bad or indifferent?

In 1985, Maurice Bertrand described the sectoral development work of the UN as 'conceptually disparate and out of harmony with the development *problématique*, fragmented, doctrinally incoherent, and operated by remote control.'[8] Much of his critique would still be valid. Bertrand was primarily interested in system deficiencies, but the more fundamental problem has been the agencies' failure to grapple with the complex nuances of field-level implementation. These cannot be understood from a desk in Rome or Geneva, or in a ministry in a capital city even in the poorest country, or at a conference in its Intercontinental Hotel – which is the closest many of their staff get to field realities. Without such an understanding there is a risk that much of the 'excellence' provided by the specialized agencies is put not into real development as it affects the poor, but – in the era of globalization – into its antithesis, activities which further marginalize the already dispossessed.[9]

'Material' assistance

As we have seen, in the early 'development' era, the UN, along with almost everyone else, saw the role of international institutions as boosting economies with cheap loans and 'technical assistance'. In this scenario, provision of material assistance – goods such as food, equipment and medical supplies – was purely humanitarian: 'development' had no role in compensating for deficits on the social side. But in order to build up capacity, and to enable basic services to function and be extended to poorer areas, governments in seriously disadvantaged countries needed practical help. When WHO engaged in malaria eradication in the 1960s, and FAO engaged in 'applied nutrition' in the 1970s – just as examples – the only way assistance could be rolled out on the ground was via UNICEF. This was the only UN development organization to offer 'material assistance' – vehicles, drugs, weighing scales, seeds, sprayers – and the only one with sizeable country offices and staff who could work with local government on field implementation.[10] (see box, 'UN spending on development').

UNICEF did have a poverty focus, on children in need – and therefore on women, families and people in need – and this was not challenged as ideologically

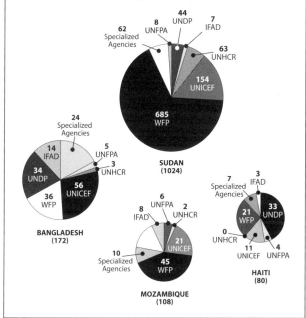

UN spending on development

The following are the expenditures of UN organizations on development programs in 2005; note that the total spent by all specialized agencies is typically less than half that of UNICEF, and WFP is the largest spender in poor countries. Some of this expenditure would more accurately be described as humanitarian aid (eg in Sudan).

UN development expenditures by organization 2005
(selected countries, in millions $)

SUDAN (1024)
- 44 UNDP
- 8 UNFPA
- 7 IFAD
- 62 Specialized Agencies
- 63 UNHCR
- 154 UNICEF
- 685 WFP

BANGLADESH (172)
- 24 Specialized Agencies
- 14 IFAD
- 34 UNDP
- 36 WFP
- 56 UNICEF
- 5 UNFPA
- 3 UNHCR

MOZAMBIQUE (108)
- 8 IFAD
- 6 UNFPA
- 2 UNHCR
- 21 UNICEF
- 45 WFP
- 10 Specialized Agencies

HAITI (80)
- 7 Specialized Agencies
- 3 IFAD
- 21 WFP
- 33 UNDP
- 0 UNHCR
- 11 UNICEF
- 4 UNFPA

suspect, either by donors or by recipient countries. Its programs were not seen as interfering in domestic policy, although they did have the problem of being tied to weak government ministries, usually Social Welfare. UNICEF also managed to stay immune to most of the accusations of padded bureaucracy, ineffectiveness, inertia and irrelevance with which the system is often charged. Over time, UNICEF grew in competence at delivering 'material assistance' within country program frameworks, and by the 1970s it had shaken off the technical oversight of the specialized agencies under which it initially operated. It was the first UN organization to employ national professional officers in the field, and to develop working alliances with local NGOs. It could act as a bridge between NGOs, government and donors; at their best, its programs thoroughly disproved the idea that targeted injections of material assistance could not be developmental.

In the 1970s, UNICEF worked with WHO to foster 'primary health care', and in the 1980s under James P Grant, one of the most impressive UN chiefs, developed a vision for revitalizing poverty-focused development across the social spectrum. The 'goals' agreed at the 1990 World Summit for Children were in every sense – conceptually, strategically, in terms of content – the forebears of the UN Millennium Development Goals of 2000, to be discussed below.

The great development debate
It would be wrong to imply that the UN has made little contribution to development thinking, despite a performance inhibited by the need to avoid interference in internal affairs and an almost pathological fear of addressing criticism at governments. Whatever they did not achieve, the three UN Development Decades (the 1960s, 1970s and 1980s – there was no stomach for a fourth), generated a series of debates about what was actually happening socially and economically in

the South, and what 'development' ought to be about. In the 1960s and 1970s, many of these took place under UN auspices.

While the developing countries were building up their muscle at the UN in the post-independence days, there was still a strong sense that there could be a unified construct of 'international development'. The intellectual driving force behind the first major protest at what the Southern economies were suffering at the hands of the industrialized world came from the Economic Commission for Latin America (ECLA) led by Raúl Prebisch, based on dependency theory. After extensive campaigning by ECLA for a new UN framework for international negotiations, the first UN Conference on Trade and Development (UNCTAD) was held in Geneva in 1964 under Prebisch as Secretary-General. Some saw this as a historical turning-point; a senior UN official stated in 1967 that the conference had 'exploded the myth that all countries are economically equal and thus established the principle that a code of rules of international trade should reflect the existence of basic differences of economic and social organization, economic development and bargaining power'.[11]

Trade between the developing and industrialized worlds, of Southern raw materials whose prices dropped, for Northern manufactured goods whose prices soared, was seen by this school of thought as inherently unequal. Instead of the poorer countries 'catching up', the gap in GNP per capita between North and South was continually widening: this was a structural fault, and the only way to deal with it was to change the terms on which international economic relations were conducted. For a while, it looked as if these ideas would gain permanent traction. The New International Economic Order (NIEO) proposal for reordering trade and investment terms was agreed by UN General Assembly Special Sessions in 1974 and

75. But when this was derailed by the industrialized world, any prospect that the UN could be used to rearrange economic (and political) power by international treaties on commodities, trade and aid sank with it. UNCTAD, which had become a standing organ of the UN General Assembly, continued to deal with issues relating to international trade for the system. But by the 1990s, it had been maneuvered into an ancillary role to the World Trade Organization (WTO), an extra-UN body in which the major capitalist powers unashamedly call the shots.

A parallel strand of thinking emerged from a group of 'alternative' economists connected to UN organizations.[12] These included Louis Emmerij, Director of the ILO's World Employment Programme between 1971 and 1976 (a program genuinely addressing problems of poverty and development despite, rather than because of, the ILO bureaucracy[13]), Hans Singer and Dudley Seers at Sussex University, and many others. Their reaction to the failure of wealth to 'trickle down' to the poor as an automatic consequence of economic growth – studies were showing that internal economic gaps were also widening as well as that between North and South – was to establish an entirely different vision of what 'development' ought to mean. Meeting 'basic needs', they declared, should be the aim and object, with economic growth as part of the machinery for getting there. Therefore, internal redistribution of wealth and building up of social capital should also be implicit. Such ideas did not pussy-foot around the domestic economic and social policies of developing countries; instead they tended to lionize countries professing socialist aims, such as Tanzania. The problem, apart from the difficulty of convincing antipathetic ideologues, was how to intervene in such a way as to meet 'basic needs' if developing country policies were not conducive.

Mahbub ul Haq of Pakistan summed up the new

approach as follows: 'Development goals must be defined in terms of progressive reduction and eventual elimination of malnutrition, disease, illiteracy, squalor, unemployment and inequalities. We were taught to take care of our GNP, as this will take care of poverty. Let us now reverse this and take care of poverty as this will take care of the GNP.'[14] During the 1970s, the UN hosted a series of international conferences, on the environment, population, food, women, water, employment and human settlements, at which the alternative vision was widely aired. The articulation of the 'basic services' strategy, in which WHO and UNICEF co-operated, was a response to 'basic needs' theory. But the arrival of the 1980s and the powerful ascendancy of neo-classical economic theory in London and Washington buried 'alternative' optimism along with the NIEO.

Re-enter humanity

Although the UN has never since contained a co-ordinated group of economic thinkers of this caliber, one of the originals – Mahbub ul Haq – eventually managed to gain house-room and a budget at UNDP, from where in 1990 he began to put out the annual *Human Development Report*. Haq was determined to place human well-being at the heart of development, and to assess this by a number of social indicators – infant mortality, literacy, basic services coverage – as well as by access to the 'larger freedoms' talked of in the Charter: democratic participation, human rights, and personal self-respect. Analysis of development experience showed that investments could be made in people in such a way as to contribute to the sum total of national advance without waiting for the national economic pot to fill up. Some countries had achieved all but developed status according to social indicators such as infant mortality and literacy spread – Cuba, Taiwan, Sri Lanka, Vietnam – but were still poor by standard economic criteria. From their experience, lessons could be learned about how to pursue development as if people, not just economies, mattered.[15] The concept of 'human development' was widely welcomed, especially by NGOs with whose vision of development it fused.

The *Human Development Report* contained a composite 'human development index' including a number of social and political indicators alongside economic growth, shaming those countries with high incomes and poor social performance (see box). The ranking of countries against the index amounted to criticism of 'internal affairs' and caused protests from developing countries that feared it might become a basis for determining eligibility for aid.[16] Despite the flak, which Haq's reputation and credentials as an ex-Minister of Finance and Planning helped overcome, the Report es-

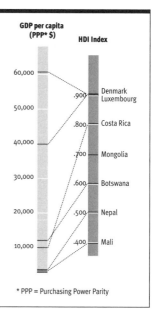

The Human Development Index

The Human Development Index (HDI) measures the condition of a country's people rather than only its wealth. The statistics fed into the HDI composite are: life expectancy at birth; adult literacy rates and gross enrollment in education at primary, secondary and tertiary levels; and gross domestic product (GDP) per capita in US$ (purchasing power parity). Since the first Human Development Report in 1990, the methodology for calculating this 'apples and pears' index has undergone endless refinement and it will never be perfect. But it depicts countries' development status in a more subtle way than per capita GDP. ■

GDP per capita (PPP* $)

- 60,000
- 50,000
- 40,000
- 30,000
- 20,000
- 10,000

HDI Index

- .900 — Denmark / Luxembourg
- .800 — Costa Rica
- .700 — Mongolia
- .600 — Botswana
- .500 — Nepal
- .400 — Mali

* PPP = Purchasing Power Parity

Source: Human Development Report 2007/2008, UNDP.

tablished itself, and so – albeit belatedly – did the idea that development was ultimately about people and the conditions in which they lived. However successfully an economy performs, if large numbers of citizens remain malnourished, vulnerable to disease, without access to education, housing, water supplies or sanitation, and their means of livelihood is fragile and under threat, 'development' has fallen short. In due course, participatory democracy, personal security, good governance and fulfillment of human rights joined the list of non-economic goods comprised in the revised UN 'development' construct.

In 1995, in response to the complaint by developing countries that recent preoccupations with international political affairs had diverted UN attention, Secretary General Boutros-Ghali issued a matching report to his earlier *Agenda for Peace* entitled *An Agenda for Development*.[17] He pointed to the recent series of UN-hosted international conferences – the Earth Summit (1992), Human Rights (1993), Population and Development (1994), the Social Summit and the World Conference on Women (1995) – as evidence that the UN was taking seriously its development mission. These conferences and summits provided settings where a new rationale for development co-operation could emerge, as a substitute for the old Cold War logic.[18] They helped define a shared understanding of the elements of good policy in various areas, and led in the direction of a new international vision of what development should mean.

The development industry – official, NGO, academic – had grown vastly over the past 25 years and become much more professional. Encompassing every issue and sub-issue from every location in the world, and synthesizing 'new international policy directions' out of the plethora of information via global 'talking-shops' was becoming nearly impossible. However, the financial crises of 1997-98 promoted a growing sense of interdependence, and a determination to find a common agenda – on environmental management, social inclusion, gender equality, food security, human settlements and jobs – that both industrialized and developing nations could sign up to. Despite its overburden of issues, Boutros-Ghali's call for a re-commitment to multilateral aid, and reforms to the UN system to enable its institutions to address the challenge of development coherently, found a response that would have been unthinkable a decade before.

The Millennium Development Goals

In 2000, Secretary-General Kofi Annan called a UN 'Millennial Summit'. The work of human development activists reached its apotheosis at this point, and global agreement was secured to focus effort and resources on eight Millennium Development Goals (MDGs). These set out measurable reductions in extreme poverty and hunger, illiteracy, child mortality, gender inequality, HIV/AIDS spread, and other development and poverty-related targets, for achievement by 2015.[19] This concerted statement of international intent galvanized effort throughout the whole international development apparatus – including bilateral aid programs and NGOs – in a way unseen since the first Development Decade. Jim Grant and Mahbub ul Haq deserve the main credit for creating over many years the underlying push behind the adoption by the world's premier international forum of a human development agenda with time-bound goals. Sadly, neither lived to see this fruition of their lifelong work.

No-one can doubt the powerful effect of the MDGs on the donor community. Since they were elaborated – and their elaboration is thorough – a whole new industry has sprung up around them: what indicators to use to measure them, evaluations of progress towards each one in countries and regions, what each will cost to realize, and which policy options in all the social

Millennium Development Goals

The baseline date is 1990; the target date for MDG achievement is 2015.

1 Eradicate extreme poverty and hunger
- Reduce by half the proportion of people living on less than a dollar a day
- Reduce by half the proportion of people who suffer from hunger

2 Achieve Universal Primary Education
- Ensure that all boys and girls complete a full course of primary schooling

3 Promote gender equality and empower women
- Eliminate gender disparity in primary and secondary education preferably by 2005, and at all levels by 2015

4 Reduce child mortality
- Reduce by two thirds the mortality rate among children under five

5 Improve maternal health
- Reduce by three quarters the maternal mortality ratio

6 Combat HIV/AIDS, malaria and other diseases
- Halt and begin to reverse the spread of HIV/AIDS
- Halt and begin to reverse the incidence of malaria and other major diseases

7 Ensure environmental sustainability
- Integrate the principles of sustainable development into country policies and programmes; reverse loss of environmental resources
- Reduce by half the proportion of people without sustainable access to safe drinking water and sanitation
- Achieve significant improvement in lives of at least 100 million slum dwellers, by 2020

8 Develop a global partnership for development
This goal provides a catch-all for measures on trading and financial systems, the special needs of the least developed countries and landlocked and small island developing states, debt reduction, youth employment, essential drugs provision, and spread of information technologies. ■

Source: UN Millennium Goals website, www.un.org/millenniumgoals/

and economic sectors to advocate on their behalf. But a very important aspect is less in evidence – one that Jim Grant would have invested his last shred of energy on pursuing. To deliver on 'goals', governments have to put in place effective planning and implementation mechanisms whereby they and their partners can actively take the MDG agenda forward on the ground, and UN donors have to provide sufficient resources inside countries to back these activities and ensure their priority. When Jeffrey Sachs reported to the Secretary-General on the Millennium Development Project in 2005, he was still calling for these twin processes to be put in place.[20]

Have the UN institutions involved in development co-operation all geared themselves to play a part in reorienting sector policies in poorer countries and implementing programs which really do contribute to MDG achievement? On their part, are developing countries attending to glaring internal inequities in service delivery and livelihood opportunities and trying to redress imbalances in favor of the poor? Progress towards most of the 'goals' is not encouraging, despite the rapid economic growth rates in countries such as India and China which have helped more people, especially in Asia, join the bottom rung of the consumer class.[21] Even if the MDGs are met by 2015 in some countries and regions, the conquest of poverty will still be limited. There is more to 'human development' than the MDGs, especially as the environmental resource base and the security of those directly dependent on it is under increasing stress (see chapter 6).

In the end, there is no such thing as 'international development'. Development does not happen in the ether, it only happens on the ground. Policy principles can be redesigned ad infinitum, but implementation is what matters. That is the most troublesome nettle for the UN and its member states and organizations to grasp, and it has been grasped far more effectively by NGOs than by their partners in the UN system. If there ever was a viable unified construct of 'development' in the years following decolonization, it is clear today that its components have to be adjusted and tailor-made to circumstances of all kinds – technological, social, cultural, economic, institutional – in each setting before the process can thrive. There can be no one *Agenda for*

Development any more than one for peace. This is an issue to which the final chapter will return. A diminution of 'international' effort, and an augmentation in the environments where people actually live, breathe and have their being, is what is needed now.

1 For a fuller account of the birth of 'international development' see Maggie Black, *No-Nonsense Guide to International Development* (revised edition), New Internationalist, 2007. **2** Kenneth Dadzie, 'The United Nations and the Problem of Economic Development', in Roberts and Kingsbury (eds), *United Nations, Divided World* (first edition) OUP, 1989. **3** *Partners in Development: Report of the Commission on International Development*, Praeger, 1969. **4** Paul Kennedy, *The Parliament of Man*, Allen Lane, 2006. **5** Maurice Bertrand, 'The Historical Development of Efforts to Reform the UN', in Roberts and Kingsbury (eds) *United Nations, Divided World* (second edition) OUP, 1993. **6** *The Ecologist* 21(2), March/April 1991. **7** *FAO: The Challenge of Renewal*, Report of the Independent External Evaluation of the Food and Agriculture Organization of the United Nations, September 2007. **8** Maurice Bertrand, 'Some Reflections on Reform of the United Nations', quoted by Dadzie, op cit. **9** For a fuller elaboration of this thesis, see Maggie Black, *The No-Nonsense Guide to International Development*, New Internationalist, 2007. **10** Maggie Black, *The Children and the Nations*, MacMillan Australia and UNICEF, 1987. **11** John Toye and Richard Toye, *The UN and Global Political Economy*, Indiana University Press, 2004. **12** Ibid. **13** Interview between Thomas G Weiss and Louis Emmerij, UN Intellectual History Project, September 2005, at www.unhistory.org/CD/Emmerij_author.html **14** Michael McLean, 'Hope on the Horizon', article in *New Internationalist*, Issue 42, August 1976. **15** *Human Development Report 1990*, UNDP and OUP. **16** Tom J Farer and Felice Gaer, 'The United Nations and Human Rights: at the end of the Beginning', in Roberts and Kingsbury, 1993, op cit. **17** Boutros Boutros-Ghali, *An Agenda for Development*, UN Department of Information, New York, 1995. **18** Nitin Desai, 'The Monterrey Consensus', in Paul Heinbeker and Patricia Goff (eds) *Irrelevant or Indispensable: The United Nations in the 21st century*, Wilfrid Laurier University Press, Canada, 2005. **19** See www.un.org/millennium-goals/ **20** Heinbeker and Goff, op cit, citing *Investing in Development: a Practical Plan to Achieve the Millennium Development Goals*, Report to the UNSG, January 2005. **21** Sarah Boseley and Larry Elliott, 'Poverty, hunger and disease: so much done yet so much left to do', *The Guardian*, 10 December 2007.

5 Human rights: the law and the prophets

The UN has provided an essential forum for the elaboration of human rights principles and their translation into international norms. This process began at its inception, but ran into the shoals of the Cold War. At its end, a 'new era of rights' was declared. Human rights has since become a major discourse in international affairs, and the fulfillment of social and economic rights, alongside political and civil rights, is nowadays seen as the justification of both humanitarian and development activity. Codification of rights, and ratification of rights treaties, provides a basis in law for pursuing these agendas. However, countries which perceive individual rights as a Western idea and resent the intrusion into their cultures and domestic affairs, have resisted. A vital question is how the UN can promote rights implementation, given its limitations in relation to national laws and policies.

THE IDEA THAT all human beings have certain inalienable rights deriving simply from their membership of the human race has a long history. The moment at which it first found large-scale expression can be dated from the flowering of philosophical thought about freedom and equality that underpinned the American and French revolutions. During the 19th century, whose many social movements included campaigns against slavery and female trafficking, the notion that there were limits on what a sovereign should be able to do to subjects under his/her/its jurisdiction began to gain traction. At the 1884-5 Congress of Berlin, King Leopold of the Belgians was only granted suzerainty over the Congo on condition that he cared for the well-being of its inhabitants. This did not stop his bloodbath of butchery, massacre and mutilation. But a precedent had been set.[1]

When the League of Nations was founded in 1919, in the same year as the International Labour Organization (ILO), the idea of developing international legal instruments to protect human beings from certain forms of oppression and gross exploitation was actively pursued. Thus, by the time the United Nations was set up, there already existed a number of international conventions defending human rights, including the 1926 Convention against Slavery and the 1930 ILO Convention Concerning Forced or Compulsory Labour. Other causes – the right of children not to be seen as 'enemy' and the right of women not to be forced into marriage – were also gaining ground, as was the articulation of 'rules of warfare' under Conventions established by peace conferences in 1899 and 1907 at The Hague, setting the scene for its adoption as the site of the International Court of Justice (see chapter 1).

Nonetheless, until the 1939-45 war, most legal scholars would have taken the view that there was nothing in international law to impede the right of a sovereign power to behave in a monstrous way towards a subject. Summary execution, torture, arbitrary arrest or detention without trial were *legally* (as opposed to morally) of significance only if the victim was the citizen of another country, in which case this would constitute in law an assault on the state he or she represented. During the war, however, a new situation arose: mass slaughter by Germany of members of its own citizenry, those who were Jewish and other groups deemed 'inferior'. When the International Military Tribunal was set up at Nuremberg to try the Nazi war leaders, 'crimes against humanity' – a phrase first used in relation to the Armenian genocide in 1915 – was included in the list of four prosecutable crimes. This was a new departure in international judicial procedure. The citizens against whom the Holocaust had been perpetrated had not been assaulted by a foreign power; so whatever rights they had had in international law must be customary, or must be rights enjoyed under the law in every civilized society.

The judgment at Nuremberg was backed by a resolution of the UN General Assembly (95(I), 11 December 1946) affirming the legitimacy of its principles, and thereby implying that all sovereign powers had to respect a core of obligations towards their citizens. To quote Tom Farer, a distinguished professor of law: 'In this way, the realm of human rights became available for general occupation.'[2] The occupying forces were diplomatic, activist, NGO, humanitarian and anti-colonial, and they understandably looked to the UN for occupational terrain.

An international bill of rights

The UN Charter stated categorically that the purposes of the UN included 'promoting and encouraging respect for human rights and for fundamental freedoms for all without distinction as to race, sex, language or religion' (Article 1,3). Article 68 required ECOSOC to set up a Commission for Human Rights, which it promptly did. But the first Director of the Division of Human Rights, John Humphrey of Canada, was under no illusion that the UN would regard it as its duty to address directly acts of oppression sheltering behind the principle of sovereignty. Threats to peace that could be met by enforcement action under Chapter VII of the Charter did not include mass human rights violations – a problem that recent Secretaries-General have tried to find ways to supersede (as already described). From the start, the USSR adopted the position that the UN should confine itself to promulgating rights: enforcement was a matter wholly of domestic concern.

President Truman in his speech at San Francisco gave a fillip to the UN's role in defense of human rights: 'We have good reason to expect the framing of an international bill of rights ... that ... will be as much a part of international life as our own Bill of Rights is a part of our Constitution.' This drafting process became the first priority of the new Commission, chaired by Eleanor Roosevelt. There was an immediate stand-off between those states supporting individuals' rights, and those that thought the rights of the group (the state) should predominate; the latter opposed legitimization of the individual's right to protest things the state did to him or her. The Commission therefore divided the principles from the actual bill under which states' obligations would be spelled out, and from the machinery for its enforcement. On 10 December 1948, the Universal Declaration of Human Rights (UDHR) was approved. The Declaration represented a list of principles governing states' behavior towards the citizen and had no standing in international law. But it has subsequently acquired a legal aura, mainly because many of its provisions later found their way into other international agreements or were incorporated into new constitutions.

Progress towards the passage of the Covenant itself was snail-like by comparison. During the Cold War, it was immensely difficult to make progress: the countries in the Soviet bloc continued to question the relevance of individual rights, and the discussion of specific violations by member states remained more or less taboo.[3] Another major difference was that the Western allies looked upon the political and civil arena as the vital context for defending freedoms (freedom of speech, religion, assembly, fair trial); whereas the USSR and its allies were more concerned about economic and social rights (freedom from want, access to health and education services, cultural identity) which in the West were barely recognized as 'rights' at all, and certainly not as rights of the same significance. It was not until 1966 that two separate Covenants – one on Civil and Political Rights (ICCPR), the other on Economic, Social and Cultural Rights (ICESCR) –

were agreed by the General Assembly.

Both Covenants contain considerable room for maneuver and interpretation: for example, under the ICESCR, the government's legitimate interest in promoting a common culture to harmonize social relations is to be balanced with a person's freedom to maintain cultural identity within the framework of a multicultural state. Under the ICCPR, a government has only to declare a state of emergency to be able to arrest citizens at will and keep them incarcerated for a considerable time; freedom of speech may also be suspended in the interests of national security, to maintain public order or support public health. More disappointing, however, was the lack of any serious enforcement machinery: states parties could ratify the Covenants under the sole proviso that they would submit periodic reports on measures taken. Despite these and other weaknesses, it took until 1976 for the requisite number of states (35) to ratify the two Covenants for their passage into international law.

Laws and norms

How international law is developed and what its many impacts are on our lives is too vast a subject to engage in here. But since the strength of any case for action based on human rights, as opposed to human needs, is that the case is legally sanctioned, it is important to understand what the passage of a convention into international law actually means. By its ratification of an international convention, a state is obliged to pass domestic laws and undertake actions corresponding to its injunctions. A convention's entry into international law means that, theoretically, a state can be called to account internationally for lack of enforcement. In practice, the influence of human rights conventions is purely normative. With the exception of the International Criminal Court, a non-UN body set up in 2002 to prosecute war criminals, there is no standing judicial machinery for bringing recalcitrant states to book. A country may be progressively shamed into compliance by being brought before the bar of international opinion – and states respond to this in some instances. The only other, quieter, enforcement method is diplomacy.

The UN has been inhibited from the start from shaming member nations because the accusation of human rights violation against a particular state may be refuted by its allies. The fact that, organizationally, the UN is built on state membership means that, in this as in other arenas, its actions are constrained by members' political, strategic and economic interests. The way such interests find expression within UN forums severely limits international condemnation of states' human rights violations. The UN has used many devices to try and circumvent this problem, including the appointment of unsalaried independent experts and special rapporteurs charged with delivering reports in their personal capacity rather than as state representatives. However, NGOs such as Human Rights Watch and Amnesty International are able to be much freer in their condemnations. In recent years the UN has recognized this and given international and domestic NGOs more of a voice in its own human rights activity.

The development of international norms may appear a weak substitute for effective enforcement regimes. But there are many reasons why the process is vitally important. Norms and treaties provide the basis for local and transnational civil society campaigns against many kinds of day-to-day rights violations taking place in countries around the world. These aim to protect or aid victims, and make life more difficult for violators. They also promote the passage of domestic legislation, which in the end is the only way to criminalize abusers – whether of the personal, institutional, employer, or another kind – and bring them to justice. 'Crimes against humanity' can today be internationally adjudicated; but routine violations against individuals cannot be addressed via multi-lateral procedures. Unfortunate though this is, it is a reality which the UN can do nothing about – except gradually push outward the realm of rights and their moral and legal acceptance.

Other key UN rights activity

Despite the lackluster performance on the two 'bill of rights' Covenants, other human rights treaties went forward under UN auspices, Cold War or no Cold War. One of the most significant was the Convention on the Prevention and Punishment of the Crime of Genocide, passed by the General Assembly at the same time as the Declaration of Human Rights in 1948. To gain the support of the USSR, the definition of genocide had to exclude the killing of members of a social class or members of a political or ideological group. Ratifications were slow to materialize, nonetheless. The US ratified the Convention in 1988, and the obligation to intervene on behalf of victims of genocide inhibited for some time the Clinton Administration's (and other countries') recognition of what happened in Rwanda in 1994 as genocide: this would have obliged them to respond to calls by UN Secretary-General Boutros-Ghali for the means with which to intervene to stop the continuing bloodshed.[4]

However deplorable this refusal appears, the fact that the debate took place, and that the Rwandan genocide was, after some delay, called by its proper name, marks some progress towards international recognition of state obligations. The genocide perpetrated by Pol Pot in Cambodia in 1978-79 was ignored as a breach of international law at the time, because the invasion by Vietnam that ended it was seen by the US and its Western allies as a more important outrage to protest. Almost 30 years later, a UN-backed genocide tribunal is finally hearing evidence against Khmer Rouge criminals, many of whom, Pol Pot included, have since died.[5] The first prosecution under the 1948 Convention was only taken out in 1998, with indictments of *génocidaires* before the UN International Criminal Tribunal for Rwanda. This followed the first prosecutions in 50 years for war crimes, in 1996 by the UN International Criminal Tribunal for former Yugoslavia.[6] This illustrates that the international political environment has to be conducive for the actual application of such instruments in practical rather than rhetorical ways. Such developments have only been possible since the end of the Cold War.

A number of other human rights treaties were elaborated under UN auspices during its early years (see box, 'Main UN human rights conventions', page 104). Some other concerns only reached the level of a declaration, but this can act as a stepping-stone to a formal treaty. These include the 1959 Declaration on the Rights of the Child; a full Convention on the Rights of the Child (CRC) was passed by the General Assembly in 1989. A Declaration on the Rights of Indigenous Peoples was agreed in 1982, but has not achieved Convention status. A Declaration of the Right to Development (opposed by the US) was passed in 1986; this was conceptually fuzzy over whether development is a condition to be enjoyed by states or by people as individuals.

For reasons of space and mental indigestion it is impossible to list all the treaties and declarations on conscience, child labor, minorities, treatment of prisoners, coercion, violence and abuse articulated through UN mechanisms before the end of the Cold War. Some critics saw the proliferation of rights proclamations as lacking credibility since there appeared to be insufficient reference to common criteria, or even to the authority of the General Assembly, thereby undermining the integrity of the recognition pro-

Main UN human rights conventions

About 100 international human rights instruments exist, including conventions, protocols, declarations and codes of conduct. The main conventions (treaties) are:

Conventions (by subject)	Year opened for signature	Year entered into force	No of parties
General human rights			
Int. Covenant on Civil and Political Rights	1966	1976	154
Int. Covenant on Economic, Social and Cultural Rights	1966	1976	105
Racial Discrimination			
Int. Convention on the Elimination of All Forms of Racial Discrimination	1966	1969	170
Int. Convention on the Suppression and Punishment of the Crime of Apartheid	1973	1976	106
Int. Convention Against Apartheid in Sports	1985	1988	59
Rights of Women			
Convention on the Political Rights of Women	1953	1954	115
Convention on Consent to Marriage, Minimum Age and Registration of Marriages	1962	1964	49
Convention on the Elimination of All Forms of Discrimination Against Women	1979	1981	180
Slavery			
Slavery Convention of 1926, amended	1953	1955	95
Supplementary Convention on the Abolition of Slavery, the Slave Trade, and Institutions and Practices similar to Slavery	1956	1957	119
Convention for the Suppression of the Traffic in Persons and the Exploitation of the Prostitution of Others	1950	1951	74
Refugees and Stateless Persons			
Convention Relating to the Status of Refugees	1951	1954	140
Convention Relating to the Status of Stateless Persons	1954	1960	54
Other			
Convention on the Prevention and Punishment of the Crime of Genocide	1948	1951	138
Convention Against Torture and Other Cruel, Inhuman, or Degrading Treatment or Punishment	1984	1987	141
Convention on the Rights of the Child	1989	1989	190

Source: Weiss et al, The United Nations and Changing World Politics, Westview 2007.

cess of human rights.[7] Since the Cold War ended there has been further activity, on subjects such as people trafficking, genital mutilation, rape, migrant worker protection and many others. A vast and amorphous array of group and individual violations have thus been embraced by human rights standard-setting activity by the UN, representing a mix of truly significant international law, along with rhetorical pronouncements of much less value.

The new human rights era

The end of the Cold War and the advent of regimes based on the principle of equality and the rule of law in Eastern Europe, Central America, and Southern Africa appeared to usher in a new era of commitment to the fulfillment of human rights. Considerable momentum was also generated by the 1989 CRC, which established in one treaty both economic and social, and political and civil rights for children as human beings irrespective of their minority status. As with the 1979 Convention on the Elimination of All Forms of Discrimination Against Women (CEDAW), an independent committee of experts was established, answerable to the General Assembly, to review states parties' reports on CRC compliance and act as an agent for international child rights promotion and enforcement. The positive climate produced an extraordinarily rapid rate of country ratification, and within five years only a handful of states had not signed up. Once again, the apparently uncontroversial nature of doing things for children obscured to many states the nature of the treaty obligations they had taken on.

While working to improve child rights understanding and implementation, UNICEF began to transform the needs-based vision of its work to the rights-based view of childhood encapsulated in the CRC. Addressing its governing body in May 1991,

Human rights: the law and the prophets

Jan Martenson, UN Under-Secretary-General for Human Rights, stated: 'The most revolutionary element of UNICEF's approach to the implementation of the Convention is the integration of [its] principles into country programs and analyses. For the first time, the United Nations brings fully to bear on its practical activities, international standards of human dignity'.[8] Ideas surrounding the evolution of development practice so as to incorporate rights fulfillment were still, then, in their infancy. But suddenly, in those heady days when the whole UN mission was enjoying a renaissance, the idea took off and spread throughout the international community, NGO and UN alike.

If the quest for 'development' had been the cause for the 1960s and 1970s, it was overtaken in the 1990s by the quest for human rights. Indeed the two missions began to be conflated. The Declaration and Programme of Action from the 1993 international human rights conference at Vienna described the right to development as 'a universal and inalienable right and an integral part of fundamental human rights'. The US rejected this position, and developing countries, while keen to have their state rights to development funds recognized, were ambivalent about any move which might make aid conditional on rights fulfillment for their citizens.[9] But rights had now become the in-thing in the international donor community, and were to reign triumphantly until the 'war on terror' began to undermine regimes of individual liberty from new directions.

The human rights takeover of development discourse has had some disquieting aspects. For example, it often seems as if rights enthusiasts think it is more important to protest breaches of women's rights in cases of violence, or breach of children's rights in the absence of schools, than actually to do something for those whose 'duty-bearers' (yes, this is the new jargon) have let them down. Despite rights education programs, many victims have no knowledge of their rights; even where they do, such knowledge is of little help to them, nor does it do anything to persuade those oppressing them to stop. What they primarily need is effective practical redress; this can include application of the law, but in most environments in the South where rights are most at risk, even if the necessary laws exist, legal writs do not run; justice systems are inaccessible to the vast majority of vulnerable people, and authorities including the police are typically seen as a source of oppression. Conventions are checklists of policy principles, not programmatic tools. However, it is also the case that programs and campaigns which focus on issues such as the reduction of police brutality or exploitative child work, based on treaties to which a country has signed up, do help improve the long-term prospects of rights fulfillment. Many such schemes, aimed at transforming minds and behavior at personal and public levels, now take place within country co-operation programs. This is a positive development.

There is also the problem identified in chapter 3, that human rights legitimization has been used by humanitarians to strengthen the case for intervention in situations of desperate suffering, also characterized as gross human rights violation. However much the case for intervention has needed strengthening by modification of Charter norms, given the resistance to human rights precepts not only by many in the South, but also by skeptics in the North, the intertwining of 'humanitarian' with 'human rights' seems in retrospect to have serious disadvantages. The melding of the two concepts has also presented problems for the UN High Commissioner for Refugees; the role of defending refugees' rights according to the 1951 Convention has at times been subjugated by UNHCR to the requirements of running mass relief operations, and some authorities see the High Commissioner's proper role in rights protection as undermined by political pressures to prevent mass cross-border migrations and repatriate war-displaced refugees as soon as it is possible.[10]

UN human rights machinery

If the organogram of the overall UN system is difficult to understand, then a diagram of UN human rights machinery as it developed over more than 50 years represents the ultimate cat's cradle of institutional confusion (see facing page). Outside the Commission on Human Rights (CHR), committees of experts (as described for the CRC) monitor implementation of the Conventions that created them; these are known as 'treaty bodies'. Under the CHR, specific rapporteurs and working groups known as 'special procedures' reported on subjects such as arbitrary detention, disappearances, torture, and trafficking; others monitored particular countries. Some involved studies, advice, or reviewing and weighing information on individual violations. In 1993, the Sub-Commission on the Prevention of Discrimination and Protection of Minorities had another 25 or so working groups and rapporteurs, including a working group on rationalizing its own work.[11] This plethora of semi-connected activity with many overlapping mandates appeared to epitomize the disease of ineffectiveness and duplication of which the UN is routinely accused; but its multiplicity was less a product of managerial lunacy than a creative response to the political obstacles facing any UN system response.

From its inception, as already noted, the CHR suffered from politicization, originally due to opposing East-West stances on state and individual rights, and on economic/social versus political/civil human rights. As the UN grew, the Commission also grew – from the original 18 members to 53, reflecting the increased membership of developing countries, especially from

UN Human Rights Organizational Structure

General Assembly

Treaty-monitoring bodies (Conventional Mechanisms)
- Committee on Economic, Social and Cultural Rights (CESCR)
- Human Rights Committee (HRC)
- Committee against Torture (CAT)
- Committee on the Elimination of Racial Discrimination (CERD)
- Committee on the Elimination of Discrimination against Women (CEDAW)
- Committee on the Rights of the Child (CRC)

Country and Thematic Special Rapporteurs (Extra-Conventional mechanisms)
- Working Groups
- Working Groups

Special Committee on Israeli Practices in Occupied Territories

Economic and Social Council
- Other Subsidiary Bodies
- Comm. On Crime Prevention & Criminal Justice
- Commission on the Status of Women
- Commission on Human Rights
- Sub-commission on the Promotion and Protection of Human Rights

SECRETARIAT
- Secretary-General
- High Commissioner for human rights
  - Humanitarian Trust Funds
  - Technical Cooperation
  - Human Rights Field Presences

SECURITY COUNCIL

TRUSTEESHIP COUNCIL

INT. COURT OF JUSTICE

- United Nations system
- Int. Criminal Tribunal for the former Yugoslavia
- Int. Criminal Tribunal for Rwanda

Africa and Asia. This introduced a new layer of politicization whose interpretation is more complex. Partly there is the same 'state/group' versus 'individual' axis; but there is also genuine resentment from developing countries who perceive rights as a Western construct, and ability to fulfill them as a product of having greater wealth and resources, more political stability, and better-trained administrative and judicial cadres. How can a poverty-stricken country provide full health and education service coverage, implement laws against entrenched social and cultural norms, and make access to the courts available to every oppressed citizen? Whatever their genuine sense of grievance, the way this has been played out in UN human rights machinery over time has succeeded in projecting a picture of Southern indifference to personal and social justice.

Members of the CHR were elected according to a formula whereby different regions each had a certain number of seats, and nomination by the relevant regional bloc – Africa, Asia, Latin America and the Caribbean, Eastern Europe, Western Europe and Others – was enough to gain membership. As a result, countries that unapologetically abuse human rights such as China, Cuba, Zimbabwe, Russia, Saudi Arabia, Algeria and Pakistan were elected to the Commission, and could block resolutions endorsing critical reports even from its own rapporteurs. The Sub-Commission had a different make-up, comprising nominees on the basis of their expertise rather than state representation, and its work was somewhat more adventurous than that of the parent Commission.

In 1993, largely as a result of lobbying by Amnesty International in the run-up to the International Human Rights Conference, the way was paved for the appointment of a UN High Commissioner for Human Rights (HCHR), and the establishment of an Office (OHCHR) to 'ensure the co-ordination of human rights activities within the United Nations system'. Great hopes were pinned on the rationalization of existing human rights machinery, and on the prospects that a senior and powerful figure at the helm would be able to exert more influence in exposing mass rights violations and making effective protests. The administrative tidying process did enable some improvements. For example, the process for requesting and receiving technical assistance in the context of human rights – for training judges, lawyers, prison staff, parliamentarians and military personnel in human rights theory and practice – was streamlined and expanded. [12]

The first High Commissioner, José Ayala-Lasso of Ecuador (1994-97), was praised by governments in the South for offering this kind of support; but Northern activists criticized the same programs because they allowed countries to emphasize positive actions while downplaying their violations.[13] Mary Robinson of Ireland, the next High Commissioner (1997-2002), was much more outspoken and critical of abuses, while earning support in the South for emphasizing the need to address economic and social rights and the 'right to development'. But in a familiar UN reprise, her public stance on US actions in Afghanistan and Russian actions in Chechnya eventually lost her vital political support.

The committees of independent experts that monitor UN human rights treaties (the 'treaty bodies') deserve comment since the way they pursue rights enforcement has become something of a model. These professionals of many nationalities review reports submitted by states parties on the measures they have taken to implement a given treaty. For example, the Committee on the Rights of the Child reviews country CRC reports, at the same time seeking the views – in the form of an alternative synthesized report – of local NGOs working on children's issues. The Committee conducts a dialogue with the country in question and issues its own critique. The CRC Committee takes the view that dialogue with governments should be constructive rather than confrontational: after all, any legislative or policy change to further CRC implementation has to take place at country level. During the dialogue, sensitive issues such as sexual exploitation can be raised. The Committee also convenes special sessions on particular rights issues – violence against children, for example. This illustrates the diplomatic rather than the condemnatory route to rights fulfillment. For pragmatic reasons, this may be the most – or only – effective enforcement process available. It does not preclude shaming or advocacy; but that is mostly done in private.

Recent reforms

In the early 2000s, the make-up of the Commission posed an insuperable barrier to progress: states sought membership not to strengthen human rights, but to protect themselves against criticism or criticize selected targets (notably Israel).[14] In 2003, Libya was elected to the chair. In 2004, Sudan was elected to the Commission unopposed, even as government-supported militias brutalized Darfur. The Commission's credibility had sunk to an all-time low at a time when the whole international community was seeking UN regeneration in the context of human rights. In 2005, the doctrine of 'responsibility to protect' gained formal acceptance, with the implication that all states accepted the duty to protect their citizens from genocide, war crimes, and crimes against humanity. The UN and Secretary-General Annan placed much store on this evolution of Charter principles, but the system's human rights machinery continued to let them down. Yet again, it was decided to upgrade this machinery in an attempt to give it more clout, and to devise a way of preventing serious violator countries being elected.

In March 2006, the General Assembly passed a resolution to replace the Commission with a UN Human Rights Council. Instead of answering to ECOSOC, the Council would report directly to the GA. The original proposal had been that members would have to be elected by a two-thirds majority and a secret ballot in the Assembly, to keep inappropriate candidates out. But this requirement was watered down to a straight majority. Membership was reduced from 53 to 47, but regional proportions and voting blocs were retained, bolstering the influence of Southern groups. The US – not in a position to assert much moral authority in the light of its own rights abuses at Guantánamo and Abu Ghraib prison in Iraq – refused to support the proposal, on the grounds that there were insufficient guarantees to keep out serious violators, and that the new body would turn out to be as ineffective as its predecessor.[15] Amnesty International and Human Rights Watch both urged approval. The US turned out to be right.

The Human Rights Council has, since its first meeting in 2006, again focused on condemning one country – Israel – and virtually none other. In the case of Sudan, whose severe human rights abuses have been documented by its own rapporteurs, the Council has confined itself to 'deep concern'. In December 2006, shortly before he left office, Kofi Annan expressed regret that, despite his ten-year effort to make human rights the 'third pillar' of the UN alongside development and peace and security, far too little progress had been made. The Council had failed to justify its creation by acting more effectively than its predecessor. He also deplored the efforts of some members to weaken or abolish the system of 'special procedures' by trying to do away with most of the 40-odd special rapporteurs.[16] During 2007, the Council's performance was as bad. During its sixth session in

September, convened just after the armed crackdown on peaceful protestors in Burma, there was an agenda item on 'human rights and equitable access to safe drinking water and sanitation' – everything, after all, has some human rights connection – but Burma (or Myanmar, as the UN is obliged to call it) was not even mentioned.[17]

Louise Arbour of Canada, the much respected High Commissioner for Human Rights, has expressed optimism about a new process called the 'universal periodic review', whereby over time all 192 member states will be assessed on their human rights record. As in the case of the treaty bodies, a report provided by the country's government will be balanced by independent accounts: a synthesized report from NGOs, and the OHCHR's own report, which will all then be discussed in special debates.[18] This process has only recently been launched, so whether it can really provide a framework for something useful has yet to be seen. Meanwhile, under continuing pressure, the Council's 'special rapporteurs' have survived and soldier on, submitting reports – on rapes in the Congo, on prisoners in Burma, on ethnic cleansing in Darfur – keeping issues in the spotlight and, hopefully, governments on their toes. The treaty bodies also extend the occupation of human rights terrain, inch by inch, by diplomatic means. The current Secretary-General, Ban Ki Moon, has underlined his human rights commitment by backing his rights envoys and advisors as strongly as he can.

Whatever valuable reporting and programmatic work on human rights different UN entities manage to carry out, the question of how an organization consisting of states can strengthen its ability to counter violations its members either carry out themselves, or tacitly endorse, remains extremely problematic.

1 Tom J Farer and Felice Gaer, 'The United Nations and Human Rights: at the end of the beginning', in Roberts and Kingsbury, (eds) United Nations, Divided World (second ed.) OUP, 1993. **2** Ibid. **3** Julie Mertus, The United Nations and Human Rights: A guide for a new era, Routledge, 2005. **4** James Traub, The Best Intentions: Kofi Annan and the UN in the Era of American Power, Bloomsbury, London, 2006. **5** Ian MacKinnon, 'Cambodia's genocide trial gets under way', *The Guardian*, London, 21 November 2007. **6** Kirsten Sellars, The rise and rise of human rights, Sutton, UK, 2002. **7** Philip Alston, 'Conjuring up new Human Rights: A Proposal for Quality Control', American Journal of International Law, 78 (1984), p 607; quoted in Tom Farer, 'The UN and Human Rights', in Roberts and Kingsbury, (first edition), op cit. **8** Maggie Black, Children First: The story of Unicef, OUP, 1996. **9** Farer and Gaer, op cit. **10** Barbara Harrell-Bond, 'Along the way home', review of Sadako Ogata's The Turbulent Decade, op cit, *Times Literary Supplement*, London, 5 May 2006. **11** See the diagram by Felice Gaer and Benedict Kingsley in United Nations, Divided World op cit. **12** Julie Mertus, op cit. **13** Ibid. **14** Secretary-General Kofi Annan, Address to mark International Human Rights Day, 8 December 2006, http://hrw.org/un/pdfs/annan_address120806.pdf **15** 'The Shame of the United Nations', editorial in the *New York Times*, 26 February 2006 (accessed via Wikipedia entry on Human Rights Council). **16** Secretary-General Kofi Annan, Address to mark International Human Rights Day, op cit. **17** Human Rights Council, Sixth Session, Draft Report of the Council, 5 October 2007, A/HRC/6/L.11 www2.ohchr.org/english/bodies/hrcouncil/docs/6session/A. HRC.6.L.11.pdf **18** 'Universal Periodic Review launched', Human Rights Tribune, Geneva, 22 September 2007, www.humanrights-geneva.info/article. php3?id_article=2248

6 Protecting and managing the global commons

Today, it is impossible to talk about development without also engaging with 'sustainability': the need to protect the natural resource base of air, climate, freshwater, the seas, species, forests and deserts that humanity must share in common. Although environmental stress first became the subject of UN conferences and programs back in the 1970s, it was not until the late 1980s, under the influence of its major report, *Our Common Future*, that 'sustainability' became an international *cause célèbre*. Two UN-hosted Earth Summits – 1992 and 2002 – have since been held, and work has gone forward on environmental protection treaties, programs, and scientific data collection and analysis. Surely, the regulation of the global commons is a task for which UN mechanisms and institutions are ideally, perhaps exclusively, suited? The contemporary test: climate change.

IN 1983, UN Secretary-General Javier Pérez de Cuéllar persuaded Norway's Minister for the Environment, Gro Harlem Brundtland, to set up and chair an independent World Commission on Environment and Development. The urgent need for a 'global agenda for change' had been called for by a 1982 General Assembly resolution.[1] Concern about the acute pressure on the environment of population growth, modern technology, energy consumption and rising consumer demand had been smoldering away since the late 1960s. The first UN Conference on the Human Environment took place in Stockholm in 1972, and launched the string of international conferences of the 1970s with which the UN tried to bring the concerns of the industrialized world and those of the developing world into unison and define a new international agenda and sense of global purpose.

When environmentalists began to draw attention to natural resource degradation, and the evils of polluting the global commons – water, soil, air and the atmosphere on which all life depends – the problem was mainly seen as relating to rich nations and the side-effects of their industrialization process. The 1972 Stockholm conference – due to the energy and vision of its chairman, Maurice Strong[2], with backing from economists Barbara Ward and René Dubois[3] – tried to link underdevelopment with environmental depletion, but the South was not convinced.

At the time, the overwhelming international concern was the 'population explosion': exponential demographic growth and the belief that it would be impossible to feed, shelter and improve people's quality of life on the basis of finite resources if the global population continued to double in less than a generation. India's Prime Minister Indira Gandhi opened the Stockholm conference by stating that, in developing countries, 'poverty is the greatest pollutant'. But she did accept the notion of a population crisis. During the 1970s, both China and India introduced draconian 'population control' measures – in one case successfully, in the other at terrible social and political cost, with Gandhi herself deposed temporarily from power. 'Population control', with its fascist overtones, has since been dropped from the international vocabulary.

In the 1980s, the environmental focus shifted. Most population growth was among poor people. And it was not they who were consuming the world's fossil fuels, depleting the ozone layer with CFCs, filling the atmosphere with carbon emissions, or poisoning soils and water with chemicals. The economic gap between North and South had further widened, and while some countries were entering the rich or semi-rich club, the trend was deepening disparity. Brundtland described environmental degradation as a matter of survival for developing countries, 'part of the downward spiral of linked ecological and economic decline in which many of the poorest nations are trapped.'[4]

The links between poverty, inequality and environmental degradation were the principal theme of the Commission's report, with 'sustainable development' proposed as the way of balancing economic growth with protection for natural resources. The report, *Our Common Future*, was enthusiastically acclaimed by environmental NGOs and was one of the most influential in UN history. But the different perspectives of developing and industrialized countries have continued to cloud environmental debate.

North vs South

The idea of restraints on the exploitation of natural resources to reduce forms of pollution that threatened humanity was perceived differently in South and North from the start. When the already industrialized countries had started down the path to 'development', no regime of international ecological regulation had been in place. If countries desperately trying to 'catch up' with the rich world against inbuilt trade and other disadvantages were now to face blocks on resource use and strictures on emissions, they would be denied a 'developed' future. 'Sustainable development' sounded to many in the South like the latest prescription for fixing the world into a state of permanent inequality between the haves and have-nots.

While it is unquestionably true that the industrialized world is primarily responsible for the mess the global ecosystem is in, the state of the global commons affects us all. But it affects much more severely those in the developing countries. This is because many more people vulnerable to sea-level change, biodiversity loss, or pollution from lack of effluent treatment, live in the developing world, and do not have the financial or technological means to handle the implications. For example, low-lying Holland has dykes to keep out the sea, but on the much larger scales and constantly shifting terrains of coastal Nigeria or Bangladesh, defenses of this kind are impracticable and unaffordable. For many years, it was hard to persuade developing countries that if they continued to emulate the unfettered resource exploitation path to development taken by the North, they would exacerbate their burden of environmental disaster. All occupants of the planet are in this together. The interdependence of human societies – more obvious in relation to environmental threats even than to those relating to 'international security' – puts a special onus on the UN system.

Maurice Strong, who chaired both the Stockholm conference and the 1992 Rio de Janeiro Earth Summit that took forward the Brundtland agenda, accepted the view from the South that they deserved compensation for the extra costs of environmental protection that they would have to withstand as part of their quest for economic growth. The way forward was to offer extra resources from donor nations. This helped to overcome skepticism in the South about global economic inequities, but the scale of these resources, what they should be spent on, and under what international regulatory mechanism, have been bones of contention ever since.

Armed with the information and impact generated by *Our Common Future*, the full range of environmental issues was visited at the 1992 Earth Summit. In the preceding years, an extensive process of consultation, documentation and negotiation took place, and an ambitious 'blueprint for survival' – *Agenda 21* – was prepared as the intended outcome document. The sum suggested for a fund to defray developing countries' environmental costs was $125 billion, well over twice the sum then spent globally on aid. The event at Rio was massive: there was an inter-governmental conference, a summit for heads of state, and a Global Forum for civil society which attracted 1,400 NGOs and 18,000 participants.[5] Strong regarded consensus-building as just as important as product, but this was not easy. The delegates failed to reach agreement on timetables, quantifiable time-bound targets, or set limits on resource extraction or emissions. Some conventions, and the statement of principles and plan of action represented by *Agenda 21*, were agreed. But the follow-up was not impressive. Ten years later, at the similarly all-inclusive second Earth Summit in Johannesburg, UN Secretary-General Kofi Annan conceded that 'the political and conceptual break-through achieved at Rio has not proved decisive.'

Bringing the nations together under a UN umbrella and getting them to negotiate, but failing to sharpen their agreements into time-bound targets, and – more importantly – failing to make member states deliver on the commitments to which they have signed up, is the perennial problem. Although the ecosystem is a global resource, delivering on its protection requires state action, and states tend to put their own interests first.

UN environmental machinery: UNEP...

When it comes to the institutional machinery through which the UN addresses environmental protection, the record is ambivalent. The management of global commons via multi-state institutional oversight machinery of different kinds (scientific, data collection, knowledge transfer, norm development, legal) has proved as difficult to construct and make operationally effective as any other. The United Nations Environment Programme (UNEP), 'the closest thing there is to an overarching global institution for the environment'[6], was set up by the General Assembly after the 1972 Stockholm Conference. It was intended to play a catalytic role, co-ordinating the environmental activities of other UN bodies (see box 'UNEP funding', opposite).

Since environmental concerns cut across every area of human activity – from public health to plant breeding, human settlements to aquaculture, pastoralism to water resource management, energy consumption to air pollution – this represented a very broad mandate. There was no desire among member states to create a strong and independent body, so its secretariat – based in Nairobi, Kenya – was relatively small and its budget dependent on voluntary contributions. Since it was ill-equipped to assert any authority over other institutional members of the UN family, it was unclear initially what it would do. Certainly, it was not expected to take over the existing operational functions of UN specialized agencies, funds and programs, or even their environmental scientific work: UNESCO's research program on Man and the Biosphere, for example, or WHO's on environmental health.

UNEP does not, therefore, undertake practical action to improve air quality, protect forests, penalize polluters of the seas, or roll back desertification, although it does help administer projects operated by other UN organizations and NGOs. Instead, it monitors the global environment by tabulating data from many sources so as to create a knowledge bank about environmental threats of international significance whose results it liberally shares. It has also played an important role in generating norms and standards,

UNEP funding

UNEP has to seek voluntary contributions from UN member states. Its situation has been financially insecure, even as the demands on it have multiplied; its lack of international influence is sometimes blamed on thin resources. In 2003, its governing council decided to introduce a 'voluntary indicative scale of contributions', telling donors what they should give. After this, income rose to $59.5 million annually, but has since plateaued. UNEP has been criticized for spending too much on advisors and consultants. ∎

Review of UNEP, cited by DeSombre, Routledge, 2006 and UNEP website.

and has helped in the negotiation and adoption of a number of international conventions. These cover subjects such as the protection of the ozone layer, climate change, biodiversity, wetlands, trade in endangered species of wild flora and fauna, and the conservation of migratory species. In some cases, UNEP provides secretariats for treaty bodies (see box, 'The Montreal Protocol, protecting the ozone layer', page 124).

With the continuing proliferation of environmental issues, and of corresponding demands for controls on the exploitation and disposal of every type of particle on earth, UNEP's international co-ordinating role has become increasingly tenuous. There are now so many overlapping environmental protection agreements and organizations of all kinds influencing state activity that the task has become impossible for any one body to undertake.[7] UNEP's position in the environmental firmament has also been weakened by the separate creation of a Global Environmental Facility (GEF) in 1991. This multi-billion 'green aid' fund was set up just before Rio as a financing mechanism for international conservation projects – to meet demands for new money for the developing world. The GEF was set up within the World Bank, not as part of the UN system. It funds through UNEP and other UN organizations, but its governance is dominated by the Bretton Woods institutions – meaning Washington and its allies, plus a few friends from the South and some establishment NGOs. This means that GEF expenditures on environmental protection conform to the neoliberal economic view of development policy and international trade, rather than any alternative, fundamentally greener and more radical, vision of globalization.[8]

... and the UNCSD
Out of the Rio Earth Summit came the UN Commission on Sustainable Development. The UNCSD was supposed to oversee the implementation of *Agenda 21* – and

'co-ordinate the sustainable development activities of organizations within the UN system' ('co-ordinate' is the most over-used word in UN vocabulary). If the mandate of UNEP had been vague, its resources few, and its machinery under-powered, the CSD was dropped into an even more complex and chaotic multi-organizational system.[9] Here, as with the GEF, the role of civil society organizations in environmental protection was to be recognized in UN deliberative activity. *Agenda 21* specified ten major groups: NGOs, indigenous peoples, local governments, workers, businesses, scientific communities, farmers, women, children and youth. The CSD was supposed to strengthen and integrate the work of all these into sustainable development decision-making, on top of its 'co-ordinating' task within the UN system itself. In the case of NGOs alone, 14,000 were represented at Rio, and ECOSOC authorized the CSD to include them all. How could its handful of international staff possibly proceed?

The CSD – after an understandable failure to follow up all the components of *Agenda 21* – began to focus its work on cross-cutting themes such as water/health/sanitation/human settlements/toxic wastes; followed by land/biodiversity/forests and desertification, in two-year 'implementation cycles'. It has managed to bring some civil society organizations into the dialogues it hosts at its periodic sessions, but its co-ordinating work among UN bodies and NGOs in the run-up to the second Earth Summit in 2002 did not impress. Observers struggle to be polite about what the CSD has managed to achieve on behalf of sustainable development, whose profile it has not raised higher on the agenda of states or organizations not already interested. Beth DeSombre, a US professor of environmental studies, interprets its weaknesses as an indication 'that it was created as a way to avoid, rather than institutionalize, action.'[10] Although there may well be bureaucratic and leadership deficits, most

The Montreal Protocol: protecting the ozone layer

The Montreal Protocol on Substances that Deplete the Ozone Layer is an international treaty to impose binding commitments on states to reduce or phase out the use of substances that damage the ozone layer. The discovery of the 'ozone hole' above Antarctica in 1985 concentrated negotiators' minds and, reinforced by scientific backing co-ordinated by UNEP, the Protocol was agreed in 1987 and entered force in 1989. It has since undergone seven revisions. Due to its widespread adoption and implementation it has been hailed as an example of exceptional international co-operation.

	Montreal (1987)	London (1990)	Copenhagen (1992)
CFCs	50% cut by 1998	phaseout 2000	phaseout 1996
halons	freeze by 1992	phaseout 2000	phaseout 1994
CCl4	not controlled	phaseout 2000	phaseout 1996
methyl chloroform	not controlled	phaseout 2005	phaseout 1996
HCFCs	not controlled	voluntary phaseout 2040	freeze by 1999; phaseout 2030
MeBr	not controlled	not controlled	freeze by 1999

A further meeting in Montreal (1997) agreed to phase out MeBr (methyl bromide) by 2005 and Beijing (1999) agreed to freeze production of HCFCs by 2004.

blame for the CSD's ineffectiveness is down to member states' lack of political will and stinginess.

Theoretically, international institutions ought to be ideally placed to provide regulatory frameworks and supranational enforcement over the global commons, as well as to adjudicate claims from poorer countries for financial and technical support for environmental assessments, and for the additional costs that protection, adaptation or mitigation measures require. In practice, the eternal problem of UN machinery – that it is built on arrangements between sovereign states, who pursue their own agendas independently of whether they share waters, air, and the ecosystem at large – is as difficult to transcend. The fact that the growth-led vision of development pursued by the neoliberal consensus in Washington and the Bretton Woods institutions is at odds with serious commitment to environmental restraint has encouraged the weakening of environmental protection activity under UN auspices. The UN is seen by the US as giving the South too friendly a platform and too easy a ride.

In fact, UN bodies, while they are more open to leverage from Southern member states than non-UN international bodies, appear hardly more attuned to the plight of people still living in subsistence economies in the most vulnerable environments. Those who suffer from ecologically damaging forms of development – large dams, for example – experience natural resource base depletion as destruction of their livelihoods and abuse of their human rights, rather than as constraints on future industrialization prospects and national economic growth. These people's interests are rarely represented by government delegations of any stamp – which explains why there is still no Convention protecting the rights of minorities and indigenous groups (see chapter 5).

An abundance of regulation

Those who throw stones at the United Nations system would do well to examine some of the technocratic activity its less prominent member organizations undertake to oil the wheels of planetary cohabitation. Under any of the major headings of environmental preoccupation – species and biodiversity, seas and oceans, the atmosphere, the disposal of hazardous wastes, transboundary rivers – the amount of regulatory activity that has been undertaken under UN auspices is vast. Without this cumulative effort, human attempts to get on in the world would be much more chaotic.

Since there is no space to consider every area, this section will be confined to just one: governance of the oceans. To begin with, international regulation concerning the seas was mainly concerned with shipping and the transport of goods and people on the high seas – areas under the jurisdiction of no sovereign state. The institution charged with governance of the seas is the International Maritime Organization (IMO). This came into being in London in 1958 on the basis of a UN-brokered international convention, and assumed the roles of previous maritime bodies. Although the IMO is another of the UN system's loosely affiliated independent bodies, it addresses any issue brought to it by the UN or its specialized agencies, ranging from the conduct of night watches at sea, to 'flags of convenience', to the unloading of bulk carriers. Currently, the IMO oversees more than 50 international agreements on shipping, some of which are codes of practice, others international treaties. These include the control of marine pollution and depletion of fish stocks, causes of increasing concern since Stockholm 1972.

One such treaty is the International Convention for the Prevention of Pollution by Ships (MARPOL), which came into force in 1978, and itemizes obligations for oil discharges and hazardous chemicals. IMO member states do not have to accept IMO-negotiated agreements, but nonetheless the states parties to MARPOL now represent nearly 98 per cent of the world's registered tonnage. The IMO sees MARPOL as one of its most important accomplishments. The agreement has fundamentally changed the way ships are built and dramatically reduced the extent of oil pollution. Optional annexes attempt to minimize pollution by sewage, garbage and harmful packaged substances. A new annex which entered into force in May 2005 limits air pollution (sulfur dioxides, nitrogen oxides and ozone-depleting substances) from ships.

The IMO also oversees the Convention on the Prevention of Marine Pollution by Dumping of Wastes. Since a new protocol was agreed in 1996, that no dumping should occur unless it can be demonstrated not to cause harm, the practice of dumping wastes at sea has declined dramatically (see box overleaf, 'IMO Conventions on marine pollution'). In 1982, after nine years of negotiations, a UN Convention on the Law of the Sea (UNCLOS) was opened for signature; it entered international law in 1994.[11] UNCLOS replaced four international treaties, consolidating all ocean regulations in one legal instrument. These include rights in and responsibilities over coastal waters, ownership of the sea-bed and marine resources, and protection of the marine environment. The part of the Convention relating to deep-sea mining was renegotiated at US bidding, although it has yet to ratify. However, many UNCLOS provisions are already regarded as customary law through their active use, and thus are considered as binding, including by the US. Although many of the institutions it has created – notably the International Seabed Authority (ISA), which adjudicates rights over mineral exploitation of the deep sea-bed – are in their infancy, this framework for governance of the oceans is well regarded, and the US is likely to ratify before long.[12] There has been insufficient willingness among states parties to co-operate under UNCLOS provisions for fisheries conservation, but this stands as an important exception in oceans management up to now.[13]

This brief account of how UN machinery has been used to put in place and administer a system of international governance for the oceans illustrates that there are important unsung areas of UN achievement *vis à vis* the global commons. Without the UN, agreement on a comprehensive Law of the Sea might still have been possible. But UN facilities and expertise smoothed the way. And this is only one area: there are similar efforts around species conservation, disposal of toxic wastes, and – a coming topic – ownership and management of space.

Protecting and managing the global commons

The atmospheric commons

The other global commons over which international governance is essential is the atmosphere. In this context, even more spectacularly than at sea, actions in one location affect many others. States cannot protect their own populations from atmospheric pollution by domestic action alone, and their own health and livelihoods may be drastically affected by the actions of distant others. This is a context, as we are all now profoundly aware, in which international efforts at regulation will dramatically affect the future survival and well-being of humanity. Among the outcomes of atmospheric pollution, the most dramatic – climate change – is a global commons protection issue on a scale comparable with no other. What role can and is being played by the UN system in response to the phenomenon of global warming?

The monitoring of world weather patterns, including atmospheric changes and levels of CO_2 (the most important 'greenhouse gas'), is undertaken by the World Meteorological Organization (WMO). This is another of the UN's 'specialized agencies' whose governance is autonomous and whose interaction with the rest of the system is on a *pro forma* basis. The scientific community first began to discuss the need for policy action on climate change at a World Climate

---

IMO Conventions on marine pollution

- International Convention for the Prevention of Pollution from Ships (1973), as modified by Protocol (MARPOL 73/78)
- International Convention Relating to Intervention on the High Seas in Cases of Oil Pollution Casualties (INTERVENTION), 1969
- Convention on the Prevention of Marine Pollution by Dumping of Wastes and Other Matter (LDC), 1972
- International Convention on Oil Pollution Preparedness, Response and Cooperation (OPRC), 1990
- Protocol on Preparedness, Response and Co-operation to Pollution Incidents by Hazardous and Noxious Substances, 2000 (HNS Protocol)

Source: Elizabeth R. DeSombre, op cit

Conference in 1979. In 1988, WMO and UNEP set up the Intergovernmental Panel on Climate Change (IPCC); this is charged with assessing the latest scientific, technical, and socio-economic literature relevant to human-induced climate change, including impacts and options for adaptation and mitigation.[14] As the threats from climate change have become better recognized, the work of this scientific panel has been increasingly projected into the spotlight. It is usually referred to as 'the UN's' IPCC, indicating that the UN tag still confers important overtones of neutrality and supranational authority.

The IPCC is essentially a scientific body, and keeping its work untainted by the politics invading every branch of international endeavor has been a priority. Its structure is intergovernmental, with all member countries of UNEP and WMO (essentially, all UN member states) eligible to participate in planning its work and reviewing its reports. But the main contribution is by hundreds of scientists worldwide as authors and reviewers of scientific literature. Since the issues surrounding global warming are politically charged – from questions of proof to questions of responsibility, from questions of impact to questions of practical response – only if the information put out by the IPCC is scientifically impeccable and indisputably neutral is there any hope that nations whose interests are deeply affected can be brought to accept its findings. For reasons of credibility protection, the IPCC may have appeared cautious in the reports issued during its early years; but today its voice has all the more authority because the legitimacy of its scientific content has earned an unimpeachable reputation.

IPCC Assessment Reports

The most important IPCC contributions are their 'Assessment Reports', of which four have so far been issued. Hundreds of experts take part in producing the different sections of these reports, and their work is scrutinized by a further intensive process of independent peer review. Each report is accompanied by a summary of implications for policy-makers, which has to be negotiated on a line-by-line basis by country delegations, and re-reviewed by experts to ensure that its science has not been compromised. The first such report played a decisive role in leading to the UN Framework Convention on Climate Change (UNFCCC) in the run-up to Rio, which entered into force in 1994. The second report provided key input to the negotiations for the 1997 Kyoto Protocol. The third in 2001 sharpened its language on the human influence on climate change; and the fourth, issued in advance of the climate change negotiations at Bali in December 2007, stated that the evidence for the warming of the climate system was 'unequivocal' and directly linked to human activity. The importance of this finding was underlined publicly and internationally by UN Secretary-General Ban Ki Moon.[15]

The Nobel Peace Prize award to the IPCC in 2007 (with former US Vice-President Al Gore) is, among other things, recognition that the UN's international institutional environment can be expertly deployed and developed to serve global humanity in an impartial, authoritative, and compelling way. In his acceptance speech, Dr Rajendra Pachauri, IPCC Chair, said: 'One of the major strengths of the IPCC is the procedures and practices that it has established over the years'. But outstanding leadership and diplomatic skills are also needed to build consensus around the IPCC's reports. In 2002, the US refused to support a second term of office for the then Chair, Robert Watson, because he was too outspoken about the risks of climate change. Pachauri, who was backed by the US, was denounced by Al Gore at the time as the 'let's drag our feet' candidate.[16] But the criticism turned out to be unfair: Pachauri has been strong and independent, and particularly vocal in support of populations facing disaster from sea-level rises and other impacts in the developing world.

From the scientific side, therefore, the machinery created via and within the UN system can be seen as a success. But what of negotiations on the instruments of atmospheric governance and repair, and – even more critically – what of their implementation? No matter how strongly the point is made that science should be the basis of any regime of international carbon emissions reduction and other responses to global warming, politics get in the way.

Kyoto and beyond

When the UN Convention on Climate Change was being negotiated before Rio 1992, the issue of reducing carbon emissions was so contentious that abatement measures were excluded. Once the Convention became law in 1994, states parties began to negotiate a new treaty for this purpose. Thus was born the Kyoto Protocol, agreed in December 1997, and ratified by sufficient states to enter enforcement in 2005. As of November 2007, 174 states parties had ratified, including 60 per cent of those deemed responsible for CO_2 emissions, but not including the US (responsible for 20 per cent of the global total), Canada, Japan, Russia or Australia (whose new government, elected in 2007, is committed to ratification).

Under Kyoto, states are divided into two groups, according to 'developed' and 'developing' status. Countries in Annex I of the Convention are obliged to reduce their emissions of greenhouse gases by a collective average of five per cent below their 1990 levels, in the period January 2008 to 2012. Countries have specific targets to reach, but may purchase emission credits from other Annex I countries. These have to be certified by a body set up for the purpose, the Clean Development Mechanism (CDM). This device helps them avoid having to make drastic domestic reductions, while generating income for emissions abatement projects in the South. Special consideration for Annex II countries means that these have no emissions obligations under Kyoto, although they can join the CDM. Instead, they are granted funding and technology transfer possibilities under the GEF (see earlier); and they can also embark on Greenhouse Gas Projects to reduce emissions, which will receive CDM-approved support funded out of the sale of carbon credits. Annex I countries can also receive credits for backing projects approved by the CDM in developing countries.

As well as expense, the Annex I-Annex II dichotomy, designed to deal with the very real economic disadvantages faced by developing countries, is the main pretext for US objections to Kyoto. As large states such as China and India rapidly industrialize, they too have become major CO_2 emitters. The US and the other Annex I Kyoto refuseniks are unwilling to accept that one rule should apply to industrialized countries – not only requiring them to cap their emissions and suffer consequent shocks to their economy and lifestyles, but to meet many of the global technological and financial costs for others' emission reductions as well – while countries such as China and India remain under no such restraint. Whatever the pros and cons, since the Kyoto Protocol was agreed there has actually been a global acceleration in carbon emissions – and not only by China. According to a US National Academy of Sciences paper cited by the environmental activist George Monbiot, 'no region in the world is decarbonizing its energy supply'.[17] A chasm yawns between what countries have signed up to in terms of emissions control, and what they are actually doing. Nations fiddle while the planet burns.

As of January 2008, the Kyoto Protocol started on its enforcement regime – a regime that will be monitored by the Convention secretariat operated within UNEP, and which can only report, not wave sticks at states parties, and even in this function will struggle to gain an independent and influential voice. Meanwhile, a UN conference took place in Bali, Indonesia, in December 2007, to put in place a framework for negotiating a new treaty by 2009 to replace Kyoto in 2012. Negotiations were extremely fraught, with the US blocking any mention in the outcome document of specific targets for emission cuts by 2020 or 2050. But finally a road-map for a new treaty was agreed, under which industrialized countries would make 'deep cuts' in carbon emissions, and developing countries would carry out 'measurable, defined, and verifiable mitigation' of theirs.[18] In an atmosphere of high drama, Bali did manage to produce what Ban Ki Moon called the vital 'political response to the recent scientific reports by the IPCC.'

In the context of climate change, as in all protection and management of the global commons, the political role of the UN is confined to providing the forums – conferences, standing committees, facilitating environment – and the drafting expertise, administrative services, and monitoring procedures for which it has developed know-how over six decades. Senior officials smooth the diplomatic process and knock heads together at critical moments. They can also make publicized appeals over their heads, as did Ban Ki Moon at Bali by flying in at the eleventh hour to plead with the nations to sink their differences for the sake of future generations. UN organizations can contribute perspectives to the debate, as did the *Human Development Report 2007/2008* in articulating the need to minimize the impact on poverty reduction efforts of emissions reduction in low-income countries, and proposing appropriate funding approaches.[19]

But in the end, emissions reduction and adaptation to climate change depend not only on international treaties, targets and policy statements, but on whether national governments implement laws and policies matching their international obligations. Whether the monitoring regime for Kyoto can do enough to bring Annex I countries into line even with their current obligations, let alone with the far higher scale of CO_2 reductions now thought to be necessary by 2020, is yet to be seen. If the will exists, then the mechanism is there also.

1 *Our Common Future*, Report of the World Commission on Environment and Development, Oxford University Press, 1987. **2** Thomas G Weiss, David P Forsythe, Roger A Coate and Kelly-Kate Pearce, *The United Nations and Changing World Politics* (fifth edition), Westview Press, 2007. **3** Barbara Ward and René Dubois, *Only One Earth*, WW Norton, 1972. **4** *Our Common Future*, op cit. **5** Thomas Weiss et al, op cit. **6** Elizabeth R DeSombre, *Global Environmental Institutions*, Routledge, 2006. **7** Ibid. **8** Zoe Young, *A New Green Order? The World Bank and the Politics of the Global Environmental Facility*, Pluto Press, London, 2002. **9** Thomas Weiss et al, op cit. **10** DeSombre, op cit. **11** www.un.org/Depts/los/index.htm **12** Lists of pro- and anti-UNCLOS arguments appear in the Wikipedia entry; in 2007, both President Bush and the Senate Foreign Relations Committee urged adoption http://en.wikipedia.org/wiki/UNCLOS **13** DeSombre op cit. **14** See About IPCC on www.ipcc-wg2.org **15** http://tinyurl.com/36jzds **16** Reuters, 'Pachauri buries Gore feud after Nobel' 12 October 2007, http://tinyurl.com/3y4n5j; article by Susan Ballard in *The Guardian*, 29 May 2002. **17** George Monbiot, 'This crisis demands a reappraisal of who we are', 4 December 2007, http://tinyurl.com/36jzds **18** For the decisions reached at Bali see http://unfccc.int/2860.php **19** 'Fighting climate change: Human solidarity in a divided world', *Human Development Report 2007/2008*, UNDP New York, 2007, http://hdr.undp.org/en/

7 The future: what chances of UN reform?

The world in which the UN now operates is radically different from the one in which it was created. The system has evolved and adapted to new circumstances, but many believe that it is in need of major repair. Efforts have been made to streamline the work of some of the core institutions and bodies closest to them, but other proposed reforms have met with limited success. In recent years, there has been a tendency to create new international bodies outside the UN system, and to perceive the UN as one multilateral player among many, rather than as the essential framework for deliberations between, and joint actions by, the nations. Is the UN concept still valid and, if so, can bodies carrying its name be made more fit for purpose?

IN MARCH 2005, Secretary-General Kofi Annan published a report entitled *In larger freedom*. This follow-up report to *We the peoples*, issued in 2000 for the Millennium Summit, also borrowed its title from the UN Charter. Five years of studies into what the UN should be doing in the new century were coming to a climax. Under the intellectual rubric of asserting the interconnections between 'development, security and human rights for all', and the UN system's unique ability to fulfill 'the imperative of collective action', this was Annan's blueprint for UN reform. The 60th anniversary year of the UN's creation, combined with the boost for international aid that culminated at the July 2005 G8 meeting at Gleneagles, suggested that a 'historic opportunity' existed for reforming the system. The package was to cover organizational purposes and mandates, the structure and workings of core institutions, including the General Assembly and Security Council, even the wording of the Charter itself.[1]

During the next six months, a full-scale diplomatic effort took place under the leadership of Jean Ping, UN ambassador of Gabon and President of the General Assembly, to develop an acceptable slate of reforms based on *In larger freedom*.[2] This was to be presented to a UN World Summit – billed grandiosely as San Francisco II – to be held in September 2005. The list of issues requiring attention was daunting: a convention against terrorism, the replacement of the Human Rights Commission, agreement on the 'responsibility to protect', commitment to the Kyoto Protocol and to the new-old donor aid target of 0.7 per cent of gross national income. In addition there were housekeeping provisions: expansion of the Security Council, changes in the workings of the General Assembly and ECOSOC, discards of defunct UN organizational mandates, budgetary streamlining, and the enhancement of the independence and professionalism of UN Secretariat staff. Consensus around just one set of issues would be difficult enough.

In mid-2005, the US was coming round to a more positive view of the United Nations following the plunge in esteem due to the 2003 refusal to endorse the invasion of Iraq. Whatever the UN's defects, unilateral reaction to international issues was not always preferable, as the US Administration had discovered; constructive criticism as a path to reform seemed to be what they, and others, wanted. But just weeks before the reform package was to be placed before 'San Francisco II', John Bolton, a fiery arch-critic of the entire UN concept and system, was appointed US ambassador to the United Nations in New York.

Destruction of the reform package

Bolton promptly set out to wreck the Summit preparations by proposing some 750 amendments to the document developed under Ping's leadership, including the deletion of all references to the Millennium Development Goals.[3] Bolton's more extreme suggestions were eventually reined in by the US Administration, but not before much that had already been negotiated was thrown wide open again and the momentum behind consensus destroyed.[4] Certain developing countries began to reassert their objections to any reform which appeared to place more power in the hands of states with power of the purse, meaning the US and its allies. At the eleventh hour, a much watered-down text was proposed by the UN Secretariat, salvaging a few elements of the original reform package but hiving the rest off to 'future deliberations.' The debilitating political and bureaucratic conflicts that frequently paralyze the UN, and the bloody-mindedness that individual states often display when asked to put their own interests to one side, had conspired to ruin the very reforms aimed at overcoming such problems.

This is probably the last time that any grand-slam effort at reforming the UN will be offered. Drip-drip reform – the way things are usually done – has reasserted itself as the default position. The web of world politics, the multiplicity of the issues, the profusion of mechanisms for dealing with them, the different sets of diplomatic, ideological and bureaucratic interests, are too intricate and complex, and the cast of characters too large and dissonant, for any such approach to succeed. At the time, the risk of Summit failure appeared catastrophic to a UN Secretariat reeling from the latest blistering report from the independent investigative committee into the oil-for-food scandal – another voice screaming for management reform. But in the end, pieces of the reform package were assigned to new committees and panels, and with some public relations spin, the Summit outcome document was presented to the world as a celebratory achievement. Even as a glass half-full, that was arguably what it was.

The story of the 2005 Summit demonstrates that, even when maximum diplomatic and staff resources are put into sensible, practical and detailed proposals to make the UN more 'fit for purpose', there are intractable barriers to overcome. To illustrate the point, there are 52 African member states, and if they vote together and 'against', this is not far short of the 65, or just over one-third, required to block General Assembly action. UN bodies were created by international treaties and resolutions of 'the nations', and only the nations can change them. If they don't like the proposals before them, they won't. What this means is that those who want system replacement or radical overhaul, and have no patience with incremental change via diplomacy, will probably have to wait for the kind of global conflagration that sunk the League in 1939.

UN reform: a long story

Calls for reform of the UN system have a history as long and as vexed as that of the UN itself. They have invariably been driven by budgetary crises: the 2005 reform package was, in part, a response to the continued threats of the US not to pay its dues. Although its previous arrears had been paid off in the early 2000s thanks to the determination of then US Ambassador Richard Holbrooke to get US-UN relations repaired, there were renewed moves in the US Congress to legislate a major cut-back. John Bolton echoed such threats in his bombastic negotiating stance.[5]

In an earlier period of UN crisis in the mid-1980s, a similar move in the US Congress to curtail the US contribution by 20 per cent sparked the creation of a committee of intergovernmental experts to examine how to reform UN institutions so that their effectiveness could be strengthened. Not for the first time, the UN was described as at the brink of the precipice, needing drastic revisions to its body politic, not to mention its many semi-connected limbs. Earlier still, in 1966, a reform initiative was set in motion by a financial crisis brought on by the refusal of the USSR and France to pay their share of peacekeeping in the Congo.[6] In 1968, a Joint Inspection Unit (JIU) was set up within the system to examine administrative, financial, and structural aspects of UN organizations and make ongoing recommendations for reform. Outside the UN, an industry of diagnosis of the patient and prescriptions for its recovery by diplomats, ex-UN officials, and scholars of international affairs has flourished: no book on the UN is complete without picking over the entrails of reform.

Out of all these activities, many changes have been made, but radical reform has always remained elusive. A cyclical pattern has become established: financial crisis and calls for reform, followed by reports and analyses greeted by resistance. After each crisis cosmetic changes have been made, but inconsistencies and contradictions within the system continue to be entrenched, and indeed are the very features which inhibit 'revitalization'. Maurice Bertrand, chief of the JIU in the 1980s, was deeply troubled by the failure of the UN to be 'a centre offering a political framework' for addressing international conflicts and harmonizing state actions in other areas of joint concern, especially economic affairs.[7] Like most analysts of the UN, he saw the ideas of the founders as utopian, made more so by membership expansion. He thought that the inability of the UN to reform itself meant that it would become ever more marginalized, while the crying need for such a 'political framework' in an increasingly pressured and interdependent world meant that this framework would therefore be created *outside* the UN system.

Despite the political resurgence of the UN following the end of the Cold War, Bertrand's vision of

The UN paperchase

Both member states and Secretariat are overwhelmed by the number of reports. This table was drawn up when the Secretary-General was trying in 2006 to offer a blueprint for management reforms in the UN Secretariat; his initial proposals were turned down by a resolution of the Group of 77. The reports listed here were only those going to the 2005 session of the General Assembly's Fifth Committee, responsible for administrative and budgetary questions.

Source: Investing in the United Nations: for a stronger organization worldwide, Report of the Secretary-General, 7 March 2006.

Report load of the Fifth Committee's 59th session

Reporting Unit	Number submitted
Peacekeeping Finance Division	45 reports
Advisory Committee on Administrative and Budgetary Questions	78 reports (15,000 pp)
Joint Inspection Unit	13 reports
Board of Auditors	21 reports
Office of Internal Oversight Services	25 reports
Office of Human Resources Management	13 reports
Program Planning Budget Division	28 reports (26,000 pp)
Other units from Department of Management	31 reports
Other departments	21 reports
	Total 275 reports in one year

...plus 80 Secretariat oral statements

increasing marginalization has been borne out on the economic front. Regional and intercontinental bodies – such as the EU and NAFTA – assumed more importance, and all the important global trade and financial negotiations began to take place within G8 meetings, the WTO, World Bank and IMF, specifically because these organizations are not constituted directly under the UN system and their governance structures better reflect the reality of power distribution in the world – meaning they are effectively dominated by the West. But on the political front, despite the rollercoaster ride of extreme highs and lows that the UN has enjoyed since the early 1990s, there is no substitute at the global level.

Even if the achievements of UN reform continue to be largely cosmetic – for example, the 2005

Summit endorsement of the 'responsibility to protect' has done little for the people of Darfur, and the replacement of the Human Rights Commission with the Human Rights Council has merely reshuffled a tired pack of cards – the work of the system in operating peacekeeping missions, monitoring elections in post-conflict environments, heading up humanitarian operations, establishing and promoting the Millennium Development Goals, leading the international fight against transmissible disease, and championing the quest for a new climate change treaty are not lightly to be dismissed. No-one would claim that any UN operation or organization performs well all of the time, and there is a real need for managerial improvement, discards of redundant bodies (human and organizational), and a reduction in the talking-shop culture, the proliferation of meetings, and the endless generation of reports (see box). But there are, as we have seen, pools of excellence scattered throughout the system's loosely woven fabric. To complain that these cannot be harnessed systematically or co-ordinated into a coherent structure is to misunderstand the nature of the beast.

Reform of the Security Council

The pursuit of realistic reform within the UN is an arcane preoccupation, requiring an extraordinary grasp of committee activities and procedures, mandates and operations, and the political and other vested interests at work. For most of us this qualifies as a spectator sport less appealing than watching paint dry, but it can be pursued via many websites and documentary sources, starting with the UN's own.

There are many proposals for improving the workings of core institutions and other bodies, but the issue at the top of every list is reform of the Security Council. The survival of power arrangements established in the wake of the 1939-45 war in the world's premier mechanism for enforcing 'international peace' decidedly needs modification. This is the only UN body where member states deliberate in which over-riding influence is vested in a handful (the permanent five: China, France, Russia, Britain and the US), reinforced with their vetoes. This has the positive value of concentrating the decision-making process and protecting the Council from the *force majeure* of numbers that would render it unworkable. But the need to include others in its upper echelons to make the Council more representative of today's world is universally agreed. Not only has power in the world undergone a redistribution, but today the permanent five contribute only around 37 per cent of the UN budget, compared to 70 per cent in 1946.[8]

Certain countries have long been agitating for permanent-member status as overdue recognition of their importance in the world. Throughout the late 1990s and early 2000s, a committee of the General Assembly debated various formulas for change, but reached no consensus. In 2004, responding to the report of his 'High-level Panel on Threats, Challenges and Change', Kofi Annan stated his own commitment to Security Council reform; but the Panel itself was unable to agree on a model.[9] Nonetheless, negotiations were renewed in the hope that Council enlargement would be the triumphant centerpiece of the 2005 World Summit package. This was also a bargaining chip: a louder voice for the developing world in the Council would gain their support for other parts of the package, such as the 'responsibility to protect'.

The High-level Panel elaborated sound principles to guide Security Council reform. These identified the need to give more influence to those contributing most to the UN financially, militarily and diplomatically, and to make the membership more representative of the developing world; also not to compromise the Council's effectiveness, while making it more democratic and accountable. These principles contain contradictory elements, and delivering on them even to the satisfaction of two-thirds of the General Assembly membership (China was demanding consensus) would be hard. But the hype about 'a historic opportunity' in 2005, along with pay-offs of different kinds, aimed to build sufficient momentum to push expansion through.

In July 2005, the countries keenest to gain permanent membership and known as the Gang of Four (G4) – Brazil, Germany, India and Japan – developed a formula for Security Council expansion. Their proposal was for enlargement to 25 members, with four new non-permanent and six new permanent

---

The veto

During the first four decades of Security Council activity the veto was frequently used as part of theatrical grandstanding in Cold War politics. In the first 20 years, the USSR used their veto 101 times, and the US never – mainly because it could command a majority in the General Assembly to which it removed issues such as the Korean campaign. During the following years the situation was reversed.

1946-55: China 1, France 2, UK 0, US 0, USSR 75;
1956-65: China 0, France 2, UK 3, US 0, USSR 26;
1966-75: China 2, France 2, UK 8, US 12, USSR 7;
1976-85: China 0, France 9, UK 11, US 34, USSR 6;
1986-92: China 0, France 3, UK 8, US 23, USSR 0.

After Secretary-General Pérez de Cuéllar instituted the system of informal discussions by SC members in the late 1980s, the style of activity changed; formal resolutions that could not reach two-thirds acceptance and would attract a veto tended not to get tabled in the first place. Today veto-holders may threaten its use, but it is rarely deployed (qv France over the March 2003 Council discussions on the Iraq war). The veto was described by Kofi Annan's High-Level Panel as 'anachronistic', but those who have it will not give it up. It has been agreed that no extra vetoes will be given out to new permanent members under any enlargement. The High-level Panel asked veto-holders to avoid using them in the case of genocide and large-scale human rights abuse, but this cannot be set in stone.

Source: Report of the High-Level Panel op cit; Source: Roberts and Kingsbury (1993) op cit

members without vetoes – to which India with reluctance acceded (see box on the veto). Of these six, two would be from Africa (South Africa would be one), two from Asia (Japan and India), one from Latin America (Brazil), and one from Europe (Germany). Immediately, there were arguments about the second African permanent seat, which Egypt and Nigeria were contesting; and other African states then jumped in, effectively derailing all prospects of success. Another model proposed no new permanent members, but a number of semi-permanent members – a 'three-tier' solution. But recalcitrance, not only from Africa but from China and the US, scuppered this proposition as well. Security Council reform was then removed from the package for the Summit, and postponed to a predictably inconclusive General Assembly debate two months later.[10]

Every year the General Assembly reconstitutes the committee to deliberate Security Council reform. Observers shrug their shoulders: if the big push of 2005 could not succeed, then how can it be done? Why do the nations so furiously rage together over Security Council make-up? Because this is about national status and the exercise of power within the most important UN institution. The more significant a UN structure, the more difficult to gain consensus around its reform. Perhaps the letting off of international steam itself provides a purpose: a case of process taking precedence over product, as in so many UN contexts. But with every new cast of ambassadors and instructing regimes, hope springs eternal. Maybe a diplomatic putsch will eventually get everyone on side for something like the eminently sensible G4 proposition of 2005.

Despite the failures of 'seminal moments' and 'historic opportunities', the Security Council survives and continues to function. Anachronistic though its constitution may be, it is difficult to imagine the day when its resolutions will be dismissed as redundant: they carry a legitimacy attributed to no other international political body. Whatever may be achievable within regional forums as they grow in significance, there is nowhere else at the multinational level where delegates can debate problems of global moment. If Council resolutions were to lose their legitimacy, a new institutional phoenix for top-level debates on 'international security' would conceivably emerge. In the meantime, the UN show goes on, and so does the Security Council at its political heart. The Council has no silver bullets at its command for redeeming the most glaring global deficiencies. But it enables the UN to do many useful things over 'second-tier' issues in countries which do not hit the headlines.[11]

Streamlining the system

In the post-Cold War period, there have been many calls from the developing world for the UN proper and the office of the Secretary-General to devote more time to issues other than those of a political stamp. These found some empathy with Boutros-Ghali, who followed his *Agenda for Peace* with *An Agenda for Development* (see chapter 4), but were especially resonant with Annan. Hence the Millennium Summit and the pursuit of the Millennium Development Goals, the enhanced focus on humanitarian assistance and human rights, and the championing of environmental sustainability. Other innovations were a focus on the travails of Africa, and on efforts to combat HIV/AIDS, both of which were taken up by the Security Council in 2000 in an unprecedented departure from standard agendas, prompted by US Ambassador Holbrooke. Such issues are normally regarded as the province of the agencies, programs and funds and do not come under such an elevated diplomatic spotlight.

Positive as it may be that the agenda addressed at the top table of the UN machinery has been thus broadened, there are disadvantages. One of these is the blurring of conceptual edges: in chapter 3, the case was made that evoking breaches of human rights instead of arguing for compassionate relief of human need as the basis for humanitarian action is not to the advantage of crisis victims. If, as in *In Larger Freedom*, the issues of political security, development and human rights are conflated – which at an intellectual level is no more than stating the obvious – then institutional mandates may also be conflated or become conceptually blurred. In an organizational framework deliberately set up with autonomous component parts so that political difficulties in one arena might not overspill into another, the assimilation of issues and technocratic areas by the UN core – even if it implies heightened international attention – has drawbacks. The overall effect is for debate and operational influence to be centralized under the Secretariat roof, when the health of the system would be better served by building the capacity of regional organizations – the African Union, for example – and defence of the independent space in which the different organizations operate.

Donor countries encourage consolidation, with their pleas for the reduction of 'duplication' by UN organizations. Superficially, these may appear to address identical constituencies and support similar programs. But this is less often the case than diplomats and bureaucrats operating in a headquarters climate may be able to perceive. Look at almost any issue in the development portfolio and it quickly becomes clear that it has myriad dimensions. Take water resources: their management affects agriculture, public health, freshwater conservation, economic productivity, extractions from transboundary rivers, protection of fish stocks, mines, urban growth, hydro-electricity and tourism; it also requires different types of activity, including data collection, research, laws and regulations, policy norms, projects and programs of assistance. The presence of water resources in the mandates of at least 15 UN bodies should therefore be expected, not excoriated as 'inefficient'.

A similar superficiality of analysis seems to pervade donor insistence on 'co-ordination'. While no-one would argue for poor co-ordination, this refrain is often a poorly informed masquerade for demanding savings whose effect in many settings is to multiply red tape and reduce organizational room for independent action. This runs the risk of compromising the quality of those UN programs that are functional and effective. While a centralized location may be helpful when issues require international consensus, it is far from being the best place to deal with issues that have to be addressed primarily in the local context. When UN organizations defend the independence of their man-

---

A typical day at the UN

The official UN Journal put out by the Secretariat in New York provides a daily preview of events. This is simplified from the Journal for 16 April 2007, and indicates the scope of subjects as well as the 'talking-shop' tendency:

UN Security Council:
Today: nuclear non-proliferation.
Tomorrow: energy, security, climate.

General Assembly:
UN system coherence for development, humanitarian assistance and environment.
Disarmament Commission (three working groups).
Advisory Committee on Administration and Budget.
UN Commission on International Trade Laws.

Economic and Social Council:
Special high-level meeting with Bretton Woods institutions, WTO and UNCTAD

UN Forum on Forests
Meeting on multilingualism (informal, convened by France)
Workshop on negotiating treaties
Panel discussion on financing development
NGO panel on system 'coherence'

Source: Newton Bowles, Alive at Sixty-two: the United Nations Today, 21 April 2007

dates, they are too often depicted as small-mindedly holding onto their turf, their quotas of international civil service posts, and their budgets. But they may also be defending one of the most important principles of UN system effectiveness: leave centers of excellence alone because systemization is likely to destroy them. Loopholes must be left in the bureaucratic web in which creativity can flourish, or everything will be reduced to a lowest common denominator of performance, with administrative processes taking precedence over products in situations where 'products' – such as lives improved – are what matter.

Under Boutros-Ghali's regime, when the UN imperialist tendency was at its height, a proposal was made that all UN funds and programs operating in the development context should be merged into one super UN Development Agency. UNICEF's then Executive Director, Carol Bellamy, fought off this proposal to subsume the various organizational mandates and identities and place them within a revamped UNDP. Instead, a more modest and practicable reform was accepted, whereby the agencies improved their country-based co-ordination, but continued to do their own thing. Some UN personnel are still fearful that calls to end 'overlap and duplication' may yet bring forth similar proposals. Only politicians, diplomats and bureaucrats with no experience of field-level realities could possibly imagine that this kind of streamlining would improve the UN's contributions to human development, humanitarian relief or human rights. The one thing that these do not need is the dead hand of centralized 'efficiency'. An accountancy version of programs, whereby the only important consideration is itemizing how bureaucrats and intermediaries spend the funds allocated, is the last thing that 'reform' should be about.

Despite the malicious rumor-mongering fostered by ideologues of right and left, the UN system is relatively free of corruption, and by comparison with most government bureaucracies, is not particularly expensive (see box on financing in chapter 1). Of course there could be improvements. But on the whole the system and its parts suffer more from centralized and hierarchical structures than from their opposite, and from ever more complex managerial and accountancy procedures imposed to secure 'efficiency'. How refreshing it would be if the UN's major contributors were to propose that a reduction of restructuring exercises and reform proposals would offer useful savings of organizational time and energy. Decay may be a more practical route to structural change, with defunct organizational limbs dropping away when no vested interests remain to support them. Take the Trusteeship Council: it still appears in the UN organogram but has not met for many years.

UN reform is too often a rhetorical exercise. Changes should only proceed where the last state is carefully considered and clearly seen as prospectively better than the first. Unfortunately this is far from guaranteed, and the political currents swirling around the various parts of the system and eroding some of the wrong ones are not likely to slacken any time soon.

So what does need to change?

If one quintessential failure were to be laid at the UN's door, it would be the failure to intervene in the 1994 genocide in Rwanda. Indeed, this case is often cited in the UN to justify radical change.[12] Many studies, reports, commissions of enquiry and evaluations have attempted to explain why the world stood by and let the massacres continue. Was it the fault of 'the nations', whose representatives in the Security Council refused to sanction an armed intervention to stop the killing; or was it the fault of Secretary-General Boutros-Ghali and Kofi Annan, then head of peacekeeping, for failing to convey the nature of the situation and not pushing the Council hard enough? Can 'never again' be assured in a similar situation? How can the buck be made to stop somewhere?

In a retrospective account of the Rwanda crisis, Michael Barnett, a professor of international relations temporarily seconded to the UN, describes how, at the time, he like almost everyone else was opposed to armed UN intervention.[13] He saw the attempt to mount a UN rescue party as an effort to go through the motions of what was expected, in the near-certain knowledge that it could not succeed. Throughout the following year, he maintained his view that the UN could not have and should not have attempted to intervene. But on the anniversary of the crisis, he saw a television program that put Rwandans at the center of what happened, and at that point he realized for the first time that it could never be principled to ignore such crimes against humanity.

Barnett concluded that the bureaucratic culture at the UN in New York generates a sense of the organization's unique contribution to world affairs which heavily colors the perspectives of those in charge. This culture shapes individuals and how they come to see and act on the world. Many senior bureaucrats have little exposure to the realities of 'the field' outside offices, conference centers and luxury hotels in capital cities. (The same can be said of academics and intellectuals: Barnett never went to Rwanda during the period of his concern.) The roles of key UN actors in international deliberations situate and define their knowledge, and inform the behavior they consider appropriate. The rarefied atmosphere at UN headquarters managed to make non-intervention in Rwanda not merely pragmatic but legitimate and proper, even in the face of genocide. Its center of gravity was too far from the carnage unfolding on the ground.

This cultural inoculation against the real-life experiences of ordinary people around the world, and the sense that decisions taken at the 'top' are the be-all and end-all of international endeavor, is the problem that all organizational manifestations of the UN have to struggle hardest to overcome. Whatever General Roméo Dallaire, the head of the small peacekeeping force in Kigali in April 1994, recommended to his mentors in New York, it was disregarded as 'beyond the mandate' or 'contrary to the Charter'. The balance between center and periphery in terms of understanding and decision-making was out of kilter. This is a problem in many parts of the system. A more decentralized and elastic framework – the structured anarchy that the founders deliberately created – has more to recommend it than efforts to bring what is euphemistically described as 'coherence' to the system. An environment which permits international civil servants to justify inaction in the face of genocidal horrors – situations the UN was invented to avert – may have housekeeping advantages, but not many others. The strength of the system is that it is not 'coherent', and some untidiness is an acceptable price to pay.

Thus, in short, what needs to change at the UN is less attempt to streamline and consolidate, and more devolution of responsibility to regional organizations and national missions with an effective and properly informed presence on the ground. This includes outsourcing to NGOs that are not formally part of the system. Although the UN looks to them more than it used to, it still tends to regard civil society organizations as junior and amateur extensions of itself, or at best as convenient allies who can pressurize member states to undertake action when UN persuasion fails. This is another cultural characteristic: a superiority complex which does not see that the most experienced international, national and local NGOs are players with complementary strengths whose knowledge and operational performance can be superior to the UN's by many degrees. The NGOs in turn often co-operate with this view of their inferior status by too ready a tendency to genuflect to grandees in the international community and borrow its language about 'co-ordination' and 'coherence' as if these were tablets of stone.

A more participatory and democratic environment for internationally inspired and funded work would be a great improvement; and it would help extend the promise contained in UN programs to the point where they genuinely connect with people's lives. At the moment, that extra step is too often missing. Instead, attention is diverted into producing yet another global report on adolescents or the environment, with synthesized, and therefore non-specific, information, and an 'agenda for action' which has little hope of realization in the diverse settings where things count.

Endnote

At the outset of this book, it was stressed that there is no such thing as 'the UN'. This complex and amorphous organizational network contains within it so many different kinds of bodies and institutional forms that any judgment over whether 'the UN' has performed well or badly over time, or in a given situation or country where many member organizations are involved, is impossible. If there is one thing that this book has tried to put across, this is it. Whatever criticisms may be leveled at the UN Secretariat, or at a particular Fund, Program, Council or Specialized Agency, they apply only to that body in that time and place. In addition, actions for which 'the nations' are responsible should not be blamed on international civil servants – or vice versa.

The UN system is primarily an institutional framework. Only in a limited sense can the UN proper, the Secretary-General, or one of the member organizations, behave as an actor in a quasi-independent role. This was not the utopian vision that accompanied the

UN's birth, and it does not meet the expectations of people around the world, then or now. But it is the basis on which it should be assessed, modest though it appears. If the UN were only to provide conference venues, scientific and technical experts, administrative arrangements, elaboration of international codes and treaties, monitoring facilities, data distribution networks and all such boring things, then it would already be doing something of vital importance. But it can and does do more.

Those committed individuals who work in the system find the constraints extremely frustrating, and spend their time trying to open up room for independent maneuver and operational clout. The prospects are greater in some organizations and offices than in others, but the current tendency is to crack down on these energies or engulf them in meetings, papers and procedures rather than to release them – a situation lamented by those it affects. Similarly, some UN executive heads have managed to open up operational space, move the international agenda dramatically forward, and achieve the kind of breakthrough in diplomacy or disease control or management of the global commons without which the world would be a poorer place. But the effort required is huge. Truly, to paraphrase Trygve Lie's advice to his successor, the UN is one of the most impossible places on earth. But it is better to work with that and make the best of the opportunities, than to disparage the whole caboodle for the sins of some of its parts.

If the UN were to sink below the horizon it would have to be reinvented. However, that is most unlikely to happen. Never mind the hyperbole surrounding some UN agendas. Never mind that most of the Millennium Development Goals will not be met by 2015, and a major damage limitation exercise will then be needed to explain what went wrong. Never mind that most of the countries that ratified the Kyoto

The future: what chances of UN reform?

Protocol are nowhere near emissions compliance. Fortunately for global well-being, the UN vehicle with all its diverse passengers and cargoes will continue to lumber on.

1 United Nations, 'In larger freedom: towards development, security and human rights for all', Report of the Secretary-General, A/59/2005, 21 March 2005. **2** James Traub, *The Best Intentions: Kofi Annan and the UN in the Era of American Power*, Bloomsbury, London, 2006. **3** Thomas Weiss et al, *The United Nations and Changing World Politics*, Preface to the fifth edition, Westview Press, 2007. **4** Traub, op cit. **5** 'US suggests end-of-year deadline for UN reforms', quoting *The Washington Post*, 12 September 2006, see www.una.org.uk/reform/index.html **6** Maurice Bertrand, 'Can the UN be reformed?' in Adam Roberts and Benedict Kingsbury, *United Nations, Divided World*, first edition, OUP, 1988. **7** Ibid. **8** UN General Assembly 60th Session, 50th Plenary Session, Official records, A/60/PV.50, 11 November 2005. **9** Report of the High-level Panel on Threats, Challenges and Change and a Note by the Secretary-General, UNGA, A/59/565, UN New York, 2 December 2004. **10** UN reform topics, www.una.org.uk/reform/index.html and James Traub, op cit. **11** Jeremy Greenstock, *The Future of the United Nations*, Director's Note of the Ditchley Foundation Conference of June 2007, www.ditchley.co.uk **12** Traub, op cit. **13** Michael Barnett, *Eyewitness to a genocide*, Cornell University Press, 2002.

Bodies within the UN system

The following are part of the **UN Secretariat**
DDA Department for Disarmament Affairs http://disarmament.un.org
DESA Department of Economic and Social Affairs www.un.org/esa/desa/
DGACM Department of General Assembly and Conference Management
www.un.org/Depts/DGACM/
DM Department of Management
DPA Department of Political Affairs www.un.org/Depts/dpa/
DPI Department of Public Information www.un.org/News/
DPKO Department of Peacekeeping Operations www.un.org/Depts/dpko/dpko/.
index.asp
EOSG Executive Office of the Secretary-General www.un.org/sg/
OCHA Office for the Coordination of Humanitarian Affairs http://ochaonline.
un.org/
OHRLLS Office of the High Representative for the Least Developed Countries,
Landlocked Developing Countries and Small Island Developing States
www.un.org/ohrlls/
OIOS Office of Internal Oversight Services www.un.org/Depts/oios/
OLA Office of Legal Affairs http://untreaty.un.org/ola/

Regional Economic Commissions
ECA Economic Commission for Africa www.uneca.org
ECE Economic Commission for Europe www.unece.org
ECLAC Economic Commission for Latin America and the Caribbean www.eclac.org
ESCAP Economic and Social Commission for Asia and the Pacific www.unescap.org
ESCWA Economic and Social Commission for Western Asia www.escwa.un.org

Other UN organizations
CTBTO Preparatory Commission for the Comprehensive Nuclear-test-ban Treaty
Organization www.ctbto.org
FAO Food and Agricultural Organization www.fao.org
IAEA International Atomic Energy Agency www.iaea.org
ICAO International Civil Aviation Organization www.icao.org
ICJ International Court of Justice www.icj-cij.org
IFAD International Fund for Agricultural Development www.ifad.org
ILO International Labour Organization www.ilo.org
IMO International Maritime Organization www.imo.org
INSTRAW International Research and Training Institute for the Advancement
of Women www.instraw.org
ITC International Trade Centre UNCTAD/WTO www.intracen.org
ITU International Telecommunication Union www.itu.int
OHCHR Office of the UN High Commissioner for Human Rights www.ohchr.org
OPCW Organization for the Prohibition of Chemical Weapons www.opcw.org
PFII Permanent Forum on Indigenous Issues www.un.org/esa/socdev/unpfii/
UNAIDS Joint United Nations Programme on HIV/AIDS www.unaids.org
UNCTAD UN Conference on Trade and Development www.unctad.org
UNDP United Nations Development Programme www.undp.org
UNEP United Nations Environment Programme www.unep.org
UNESCO UN Educational, Scientific and Cultural Organization www.unesco.org
UNFIP UN Fund for International Partnerships www.un.org/unfip/
UNFPA UN Population Fund www.unfpa.org

UN-HABITAT UN Human Settlements Programme www.unhabitat.org
UNHCR Office of the UN High Commissioner for Refugees www.unhcr.org
UNICEF UN Children's Fund www.unicef.org
UNICRI UN Interregional Crime and Justice Research Institute www.unicri.it
UNIDIR UN Institute for Disarmament Research www.unidir.org
UNIDO UN Industrial Development Organization www.unido.org
UNITAR UN Institute for Training and Research www.unitar.org
UNMOVIC UN Monitoring, Verification and Inspection Commission
    www.unmovic.org
UNODC UN Office on Drugs and Crime www.unodc.org
UNOG UN Office at Geneva www.unog.ch
UNON UN Office at Nairobi www.unon.org
UNOPS UN Office for Project Services www.unops.org
UNOV UN Office at Vienna www.unvienna.org
UNRISD UN Research Institute for Social Development www.unrisd.org
UNRWA UN Relief and Works Agency www.un.org/unrwa/
UNSECOORD Office of the UN Security Coordinator
UNSSC UN System Staff College www.unssc.org
UNU UN University www.unu.edu
UNV UN Volunteers www.unv.org
UNWTO World Tourism Organization www.world-tourism.org
UPU Universal Postal Union www.upu.int
WFP World Food Programme www.wfp.org
WHO World Health Organization www.who.int
WIPO World Intellectual Property Organization www.wipo.int
WMO World Meteorological Organization www.wmo.ch

Index

Index

Index